U0508185

名师名校名校长

凝聚名师共识
囿志名师关怀
打造名师品牌
培育名师群体

初中英语教学中学生评判性思维能力的培养研究

潘洪翠　赖丽萍　著

西安出版社

图书在版编目（CIP）数据

初中英语教学中学生评判性思维能力的培养研究 /
潘洪翠，赖丽萍著.—西安：西安出版社，2023.12
ISBN 978-7-5541-7308-4

Ⅰ.①初… Ⅱ.①潘… ②赖… Ⅲ.①英语课—教学
研究—初中 Ⅳ.①G633.412

中国国家版本馆CIP数据核字（2024）第016433号

初中英语教学中学生评判性思维能力的培养研究
CHUZHONG YINGYU JIAOXUE ZHONG XUESHENG PINGPANXING SIWEI NENGLI DE PEIYANG YANJIU

出版发行：西安出版社
社　　址：西安市曲江新区雁南五路 1868 号影视演艺大厦 11 层
电　　话：（029）85264440
邮政编码：710061
印　　刷：北京政采印刷服务有限公司
开　　本：787mm×1092mm　1 / 16
印　　张：13.25
字　　数：204千字
版　　次：2023 年 12 月第 1 版
印　　次：2024 年 5 月第 1 次印刷
书　　号：ISBN 978-7-5541-7308-4
定　　价：58.00 元

△本书如有缺页、误装等印刷质量问题，请与当地销售商联系调换。

前　言

　　本书是基于市级研究课题"学科核心素养视角下初中英语阅读教学对学生评判性思维的促进作用"而著。感谢课题组全体成员认真研究，并提供相关数据支持。

　　本书以外语教学流派中的"认知法"理论和建构主义理论为基础，依托文秋芳层级理论模型和布鲁姆的教育目标分类法设计研究计划，展开行动研究。该研究经历了两轮教学实践，通过对比前后问卷、访谈和前测与后测等数据，得出结论：通过优化教学活动的设计能提高学生的阅读兴趣，促进其评判性思维的发展，同时，不同水平学生的阅读能力均有提高，尤其是中高级水平的学生。

　　本书为初中英语阅读教学中学生思维品质的培养之评判思维能力的培养提供了相关数据参考，总结了研究取得的一些成果。

　　（1）在初中英语阅读教学中培养学生评判性思维能力的六个教学策略：①利用读前预测与假设活动，融合学生已有知识，学习阅读图示的方法，培养其推测能力等；②通过对学生的预测结果和阅读文章的结构及主旨大意的对比，帮助学生形成新的阅读图式，培养其评判能力；③指导学生用思维导图的方式梳理文章脉络，更有利于学生评判性思维能力的培养；④在细节阅读的研读文本推理解释活动中，教师通过巧妙设计问题链，培养学生的分析、解释和评价能力；⑤通过读后的自评活动，帮助学生读中专注，读后反思，培养其自我监控能力；⑥在作业设计环节，教师通过让学生模仿写作、篇章创作，或故事续写等形式，培养学生的创新应用能力。

（2）用流程图的形式展示了四种体裁评判性阅读教学流程。

（3）可以促进学生评判性思维发展的问题。例如，解释与分析类：Which character do you like? Why? 分析与推理类：What can you infer from ...?

本书只是课题研究的一家之言，由于作者水平有限，难免存在疏漏及不足的地方，敬请读者批评指正。

目录

上 篇
评判性阅读教学的研究理论与实践

下 篇
评判性阅读教学设计案例

附　录

上 篇

评判性阅读教学的
研究理论与实践

第一章　培养学生评判性思维的研究背景

在世界飞速发展、科技进步日新月异的背景下，知识以几何倍数无穷尽增长，很多工作也即将被人工智能所取代，教育本身不能将无穷尽的知识全部教授给学生，知识更新的速度也不可估量。未来的世界需要的人才不再是知识型人才，而是具有批判性、能创造性地解决问题、有创新能力的人才。而英语作为一门语言，它本身就是思维的一种工具，也是人们思想交流的工具。思维是语言的核心要素，那么，如何在英语的教与学中发展学生的思维，让其成为终身受用的财富呢？怎样的教育才能让学生结束受教育后仍受益终身？这些问题一直萦绕在笔者脑海中。

王蔷（2015）在中国教育学会外语教育专业委员会第19次学术年会上所作的主旨发言中指出，英语学科核心素养由语言能力、思维品质、文化意识和学习能力四方面构成。她指出，"通过感知、预测、获取、分析、概括、比较、评价、创新等思维活动，在分析问题和解决问题的过程中发展思维品质，促进英语学科核心素养的形成和发展"。而后，程晓堂、赵思齐（2016）详述了英语学科核心素养的实质内涵，在思维品质方面特指与英语学习紧密相关的一些思维品质，如根据所学概念性英语词语和表达句式，学会从不同角度思考和解决问题；根据所给信息提炼事物共同特征，借助英语形成新的概念。

受到专家的启发，结合对平时教学的思考，笔者开始研读一些有关思维品质培养的专业书籍或已发表的文章。其间研读了*A Taxonomy for Learning, Teaching, and Assessing: Pearson New International Edition*、《布卢姆教育目标分类学：分类学视野下的学与教及其测评（完整版）（修订版）》、《批判性思维（原书第10版）》、《中学英语教师阅读教学研究丛书·英语阅读教学中的问题设计：评判性阅读视角（第2版）》等书，于是聚焦到了思维品质中评判性思维（Critical Thinking）能力的研究。评判性思维是思维能力的重要组成部分，其基本内涵是：运用恰当的评价标准，进行有意识的思考，最终做出有理据的判断（转引自文秋芳，2012）。评判性思维的概念最初起源于20世纪30年代约翰·杜威的反思性思维（Reflective Thinking）。杜威认为，思维缺乏反思意义不太重大，对于一系列的想法还需要一定的顺序和确定的结果作为正确想法。之后，Glaser（1941）认为个人的态度倾向也是运用评判性思维的一个重要方面。Dressel和Mayhew（1954）认为评判性思维是一种能筛选信息、进行假设并且检验实施，最终确认正确结论的能力。Ennis（1989）则认为评判性思维是经过慎重考虑、检验反思性思维后确定什么值得相信的反省思维。

Facione（1990）在特尔斐报告中指出："批判性思维是有目的的、通过自我校准的判断。这种判断可以表现为解释、分析、评价、推断以及判断存在的论据、概念、方法、标准或语境的说明。"Halpern（2001）认为批判性思维是分析、整合、评价信息的能力以及运用这些能力的倾向。特尔斐项目构建了思辨能力的双维结构模型，Richard Paul（2008）也构建了三元结构模型。

国内将Critical Thinking翻译成批判性思维，或评判性思维，或思辨能力。本书采用评判性思维的称谓。美国哲学学会认为评判性思维包括认知技能（cognitive skills）和情感特质（affective dispositions）。核心评判性思维技能包括：解释（interpretation）——包括归类、阐明重要性和澄清意义；分析（analysis）——审查理念、发现论证和分析论证及其成分；评估（evaluation）——评估主张、评估论证；推论（inference）——质疑证据，提出猜想和推出结论；说明（explanation）——陈述结果、证明程序的正当性和表达论证；自我校准（self-regulation）——自我审查和自我校正。

为了实际测量学生的评判性思维能力，学者研究制定出超过20种测量方式，如加利福尼亚评判技能量表（California Critical Thinking Skills Test，CCTST）、加利福尼亚评判倾向问卷（Critical Thinking Disposition Inventory，CCTDI）、剑桥思维能力测试（Cambridge Thinking Skills Assessment，CTSA）。

近年来，从思维的角度研究英语阅读的文章不断涌现。在国外，Mohammad Taghi Hassani、Ramin Rahmani等调查了伊朗EFL学习者的评判性思维与期刊文本阅读理解之间的关系。通过一个评判性思维问卷和一个测量阅读理解能力的新闻测验，以找出评判性思维与阅读理解新闻文本之间的关系。结果显示两个变量之间存在强相关性，对提高EFL学习者阅读新闻文本的能力具有理论和实践意义。Mansoor Fahim（2010）利用"沃森-格拉泽评判性思维评价表"和托福阅读题目分析得出托福阅读部分的表现与评判性思维能力之间显著正相关。此外，研究发现托福阅读部分有三种类型的问题，即词汇、连贯性和阅读理解项目，评判性思维对于回答阅读理解问题尤为重要，尤其是与主要思想相关的。2012年，Mohammad Reza Talebinezhad和Zahra Matou调查了所用的课程书籍，以了解在这些书籍中提倡评判性思维的程度。研究证实了评判性思维能力与阅读理解之间存在正相关关系，探讨伊朗大学一级阅读理解教材中使用评判性思维的频率。课程的练习或问题可以被认为是促进评判性思维的有效手段。

国内关于评判性思维的研究也方兴未艾。中国知网检索结果显示，英语阅读批判性或评判性思维培养总共387篇论文，在大学教学中的研究论文有80篇，高中部分84篇，初中部分21篇。高等教育阶段研究占总研究的21%，高中阶段研究占22%，初中阶段研究占5%，证明该领域的研究在教育领域所占比重较大，并且以大学和高中为主，初中阶段的研究严重缺乏。2017年该领域发表35篇论文，2018年54篇，2019年62篇，呈逐年上升的趋势，越来越多的教师和学者都开始关注并致力于该领域的研究。

国内关于思维品质的研究主要集中于探究思维能力培养的策略。欧文勤（2012）等学者对思维品质的性质特征以及培养策略进行了总体的分析。潘叶飞（2011）指出良好的思维品质对英语阅读教学具有促进作用，并且提出了思维品质的培养模式，包括立足课本、创设情境、以问导学和精泛结合等。冀小婷（2016）从政策指导、教师、教学活动三个层面对英语学科核心素养培养的实现途径进行了论述，列举阅读、口语、写作课型的活动建议，以培养学生语言能力、思维品质、文化品格和学习能力。

此外，张若兰（1996）在《英语精读教学中的思维训练》一文中，从设疑激发思维兴趣、活用课本培养思维方法、实践优化思维品质三方面探讨了大学英语精读教学中的思维训练，她指出不管哪一种体裁的文章，都要运用分析与综合、抽象与概括、判断与推理等基本的思维方法。张旭（2016）以高中英语人教版选修八Unit 3的阅读课设计为例，指出教师要在导入、读前、读中、读后以及作业布置五个环节设计有利于发展学生思维品质的活动，渗透文化意识。章策文（2016）在分析了高中英语阅读课堂中存在的教学模式固化、文本理解浅表化、活动设置形式化等现状之后，指出教师要根据学生特点，科学地设置开放式问题，引导学生赏析和鉴别语言，学会思考。李杰（2013）阐述了思维品质在阅读理解中的重要性，并指出启发拓展、限时训练、多重变式等方法来培养思维品质。在小学阶段，宋惠芳（2017）表明要充分挖掘教材，结合学生实际，把思维培养和语言教学融合起来。其他学者则从课堂提问这一具体的角度来探究思维品质的培养。如戴聪萍（2017），基于思维品质培养，探究高中英语阅读教学的设问技巧，通过读前巧问、读中追问、读后反问的设问方式来培养学生的思维品质，进而提升英语学科核心素养。在《英语课堂中基于提问的思维品质培养》一文中，王式街（2015）借助不同时机的提问、问题链和教材中的问题来培养学生思维的深刻性、灵活性、独创性、评判性和敏捷性等不同品质。

董焱（2017）在《基于批判性思维子技能的高中英语阅读教学设计思考》一文中根据文章体裁、写作目的、上下文语境的思维示意图对文本进行解读，评价时可以指向其来源是否可靠、推理过程是否合理、论断是否客观站得住脚。易荣楣（2017）在《利用英语阅读文本，培养中学生批判性思维能力》一文中探讨了评判性思维培养的缘由、培养评判性思维的理论基础以及在中学阅读教学中培养评判性思维的途径。景晶（2018）从提高高中英语词汇教学的有效性角度加强对学生评判性思维能力的培养，改变高中英语阅读课的传统模式，侧重分析、评价等深层问题。

以上研究大部分都基于某一种教材的不同单元，鲜有研究从不同体裁探讨培养评判性思维的策略，以及初中英语阅读课具体在什么环节采用什么教学策略培养学生的评判性思维。

文秋芳教授将"Critical Thinking"界定为"高层次思维能力"，后来用"高层次思辨能力"或"思辨能力"来表达这个英文词组。在双维模型、三元模型和三棱模型的基础上，文秋芳提出层级模型。其层级理论模型分为元思维能力和思维能力两个层面。

元思维能力主要指自我调控能力，是对自己思维进行计划、检查、调整与评估的技能。思维能力即思辨能力，它包含三项认知技能和五项情感态度。其中，认知技能是指分析、推理、评价的技能。分析是对事物进行了解、判断，并给出客观全面深入的描述，客观呈现事物本身及其发展。推理是根据一定的逻辑关系，对事物的走向或是细节态度的推测。评价即根据某些标准、已有的经验以及主观的喜好对事物进行预测或者评判。这三种技能同时需要五项认知标准进行规范、深化，才能实现思维的评判性。这五项标准分别是精晰性、相关性、逻辑性、深刻性与灵活性，即分析、推理、评价必须精确、清晰，切合问题的主题，突出重点，逻辑清晰，有理有据，体现深度和广度，避免浮于表面，同时灵活转换，根据具体场景和思维方式随时切换技能。

该研究主要集中于大学和高中阶段，基本采用提问的方式训练学生的评判性思维。实施通常分为三个阶段：初级阶段、提高阶段和高级阶段。教师通过苏格拉底问答法、讨论式教学法、探究式教学法等方法设计不同层次的问题，如在文中能找到答案的基础事实性问题、需要在文中找线索进行推理的问题、开放式的问题，引导学生发散思维、让学生学会质疑、提升学生思维品质，培养评判性思维，更加自主学习。实施阶段和方法见表1-1。

表1-1　文秋芳层级理论实施阶段和方法

实施阶段	初级阶段	提高阶段	高级阶段
培养目标	分析能力	推理能力	评价能力
教学方法	苏格拉底问答法	讨论式教学法	探究式教学法
教学实践	教师设计问题、提出问题：答案具有开放性；学生协作、自主分析	教师分配小组和个人任务；小组分工合作；学生在论辩冲突中探究与推理	教师适当引导，学生思考与探究：提出个人观点：分析、推理基础上给予评价

已有的论文均从提问策略研究、课程设计方式、量化工具的使用方面对评判性思维的培养做出了研究，但研究缺乏对初中阶段阅读教学的探索与实践。初中生英语水平相对薄弱，但评判性思维对学生长期的学习能力发展非常有帮助，越早开始训练，学生越早受益，越能形成自主评判力和学习力，从而实现高效学习。

2018年1月《普通高中英语课程标准（2017年版）》发布，新课标明确指出，学科核心素养是学科育人价值的集中体现，是学生通过学科学习而逐步形成的正确价值观念、必备品格和关键能力。英语学科核心素养主要包括语言能力、文化意识、思维品质和学习能力四个维度。英语语言能力构成英语学科核心素养的基础要素。文化意识体现英语学科核心素养的价值取向。学习能力构成英语学科核心素养的发展条件。思维品质指思维在逻辑性、评判性、创新性等方面所表现的能力和水平。思维品质体现英语学科核心素养的心智特征。思维品质的发展有助于提升学生分析和解决问题的能力，使他们能够从跨文化视角观察和认识世界，对事物作出正确的价值判断。思维品质的目标就是学习者能辨析语言和文化中的具体现象，梳理、概括信息，构建新概念，分析、推断信息的逻辑关系，正确评判各种思想观点，创造性地表达自己的观点，具备多元思维的意识和创新思维的能力（教育部，2018）。自《普通高中英语课程标准（2017年版）》明确英语学科素养包含思维品质以来，思维品质尤其是评判性思维的研究与实践得到了广泛的关注。

但在初中英语阅读教学的实践中仍然存在以下不利于培养学生评判性思维的情况：教学重点在词汇、句型等语言知识的理解和记忆上，缺乏根据上下文语境分析推理的活动；偏重对文本基本信息的提取和获得，忽略对作者写作意图与观点的分析；没有给学生充分的阅读与思考的时间，缺乏对文本本身的深层解读及对文本的架构与逻辑合理性评判的活动；在讨论和表述观点的活动中，教师预设答案，学生的观点只有与其预设答案相似或吻合才算正确，限制了学生的想象力与思维活跃性；阅读教学之后的作业设计与阅读课无关联，不利于学生评判性思维的深刻性与延续性的培养。

学科核心素养的要求和以上实际问题的出现，增强和坚定了笔者要研究评判性思维的信心。于是，申请并通过了深圳市教育科学院的题为"学科核心素养视角下初中英语阅读教学对学生批判性思维的促进作用"的课题研究，确定了三个研究问题：阅读教学设计的优化是否能促进学生评判思维的发展，不同水平学生表现如何？阅读教学设计的优化是否有助于提高学生的阅读能力？初中英语阅读教学中促进学生评判性思维发展的教学策略有哪些，在不同体裁的文本中是如何体现的？课题组围绕以上问题进行了为期两年的教学实践。

本书从优化阅读教学设计的角度探讨评判性思维能力的培养，主要通过课例的形式进行了研究，具有可操作性。我们的研究主要有以下特点。

（1）基于常态阅读课，融入研究主题。

（2）采用行动研究法。我们经过一次次的课例改进，记录下过程中的做法、课堂实录并进行了反思，再调整设计、实录、再反思，最终形成比较可行的教学课例。

（3）质的研究和量的研究相互印证。为了使课题具有客观性，提高可信度，本课题除了采用问卷调查、访谈、反思等手段，还对研究对象进行了前测、中测和后测，并使用SPSS分析工具对前、中、后测成绩进行了数据分析。

对于本课题的研究，我们经历了以下的过程。

（1）感知理念：《普通高中英语课程标准（2017年版）》发布之后，我们认为培养学生的思维品质非常重要，而评判性思维是一个非常先进的理念，就选定它作为课题组今后努力的方向，但对于具体如何把理念融入我们平时的教学，研究的主要内容应聚焦在哪些方面等问题仍然很迷茫。

（2）确定方向：通过阅读大量文献，基本了解了评判性思维的定义、由来、分类、内容、测量工具，我们有了豁然开朗的感觉，也更加确定我们的研究方向是可行的、有意义的。

（3）聚焦问题：作为一线初中英语教师，我们的课本主要是阅读文本，那么我们就聚焦到如何在平时教学中落实评判性思维的培养，而且我们能做的就只有教学实践研究，因此，最终聚焦到如何优化教师的阅读教学设计去培养学生的评判性思维。

（4）深入研究：我们通过剖析一个个的评判性思维培养的教学案例，发现问题后，通过多次研讨、优化，提炼出评判性思维能力培养的关键策略。

（5）总结：我们对研究中的各项数据、实践方法、策略应用进行总结反思，最后形成一套可以推广的教学设计案例集，可供同行参考。

第二章 培养学生评判性思维能力的研究理论和过程设计

一、核心概念的界定

（一）评判性思维

根据Paul和Elder的论述，评判性思维是指"运用恰当的评价标准，进行有意识的思考，最终做出有理据的判断"（转引自文秋芳，2012）。学生评判性思维的水平取决于他们在解决问题过程中表现出来的解读、分析、推理、评价、解释和自我监控能力的高低（包丰，2019）。

（二）阅读与阅读教学

阅读是一项复杂的认知活动，是读者利用来自文本材料的信息，从语言材料中提取信息，通过与自己大脑中的已有知识相结合，建构意义的过程。读者阅读文本时一般涉及三种信息加工活动：首先是句子层面的词句解码活动，然后是段落或宏观命题层面的组织活动，最后是整体语篇结构的分析综合活动。根据对阅读的不同理解，人们提出了以下几种阅读模式。

1. 文本驱动模式

文本驱动模式就是自下而上的阅读。读者首先理解字母和单词，然后理解短语、句子和段落，最后理解语篇。

2. 图式驱动模式

图式驱动模式认为阅读是一种心理猜测过程。与文本驱动模式不同，图式驱动阅读认为理解涉及文本和图式两方面的因素，读者在进行文本解码的同时，也在应用其已有的知识，帮助理解，如世界知识、文化知识、话题知识、语篇知识、策略知识等。读者可以对正在阅读的材料和接下来要阅读的材料进行猜测，而整个阅读过程就是猜测、预测、验证预测、修正预测、调整预测的过程，因此阅读就是读者与文本的交互对话过程。

3. 交互阅读模式

交互阅读模式认为阅读是一个交互过程。主要有两点：一是读者与文本的交互；二是文本驱动与图式驱动的交互。读者对文本信息的建构部分依赖于文本信息，部分依赖于读者已有的相关知识。要理解文本信息，读者不仅要掌握解码技能，还必须掌握应有的知识。读者的解码技能与图式互补，帮助读者更好地理解所读材料（王笃勤，2012）。

本研究采用的是交互阅读模式，学生在阅读过程中依赖文本信息和已有的相关话题图式，对阅读文章进行解码，对原有图式进行修正，并形成新的阅读图式。同时，在课堂阅读教学模式方面，本研究采用的是PWP阅读教学模式。

PWP阅读教学模式指将阅读教学分为pre-reading，while-reading和post reading三段教学的一种阅读教学模式，其教学目标与教学活动在三个阶段有着各自的特点。读前教学（pre-reading）的核心任务就是为阅读做准备。读前的准备主要包括背景图式的激活、话题的导入、任务的介绍、兴趣的激发和语言策略准备。读中教学（while-reading）是阅读教学的核心，各种阅读能力的培养都是通过读中阶段的教学完成的。从具体信息的识别，到推理判断能力的培养，再到各种逻辑关系、篇章结构的分析，阅读能力中的知识层面、理解层面、分析层面一般都在读中阶段完成。读后教学（post-reading）侧重于对作者意图、文章结构、篇章观点等的评价或角色代入深入理解人物特点、学习效果自我评价等。

（三）阅读能力

外语阅读主要是通过解码文本中的语言符号、从文本中提取信息、运用认知和各种加工策略，同时调动自身的背景知识或认知图式来理解文本的过程。因此外语阅读能力包含解码能力、理解信息的能力以及运用认知和元认知策略的能力。

解码能力指学生对读物的外观、文字、音素、图片等基本信息的意义抓取和理解的能力，具体包括文本概念、音素意识、拼读能力和阅读流畅度四个要素。语言知识是解码能力发展的基础，包括词汇知识、语法知识和语篇知识三个要素。阅读理解即读者对读物的理解与信息的运用，是整个阅读能力的核心，包括信息提取、策略运用和多元思维三个要素，具体包含抓取特定信息，运用概括、分类、归纳、比较等多种策略，经过评判性思维，在阅读过程中对作者的观点、写作技巧、插图的使用等做出个人的评价和简介，能够从不同的方面进行比较和鉴赏，同时也能接受他人不同的观点和看法，或者是学生通过阅读大量作品，发现文本与文本之间的关联，能够从宏观的角度对这些具有关联的文本进行分析、比较和评论。

二、理论基础与依托理论

（一）理论基础

本研究基于外语教学流派中的"认知法"理论和建构主义理论。认知法又叫认知符号法，注重学生的智力因素，强调理解在外语教学中的作用，主张在理解的基础上培养学生的语言交际能力，反对类似视听法等教学法的机械操作，以听说法的对立面而产生。认知法的主要特点有：在理解的基础上学习语言；同时发展听、说、读、写技能；注重培养交际能力。认知法注重学生的智力因素，鼓励学生积极思维，但作为一种教学体系，仍需要在理论和实践上进一步充实。

同时，建构主义学习理论有以下几个观点。

（1）学习是一个积极主动的建构过程。学习者不是被动地接受外在信息，而是根据先前认知结构主动地和有选择性地知觉外在信息，建构当前事物的意义。

（2）知识是个人经验的合理化，而不是说明世界的真理。因为个体先前的经验毕竟是十分有限的，在此基础上建构知识的意义，无法确定所建构出来的知识是否就是世界的最终写照。

（3）知识的建构并不是任意的和随心所欲的。建构知识的过程必须与他人磋商并达成一致，并不断地加以调整和修正，在此过程中，不可避免地要受到当时社会文化因素的影响。

（4）学习者的建构是多元化的。由于事物存在复杂多样化，学习情感存在一定的特殊性，以及个人的先前经验存在独特性，每个学习者对事物意义的建构都是不同的。

（二）依托理论

1. 文秋芳层级理论模型

文秋芳教授在国外Critical Thinking的基础上提出层级理论模型，将之界定为高层次思维能力，又分为元思维能力和思维能力。元思维能力主要指自我调控能力，是对自己思维进行计划、检查、调整与评估的技能。思维能力包括认知能力和情感特质，其中认知能力又包含分析、推理、评价三项技能。期望思维者能够进行归类、识别、比较、澄清、区分、阐释等活动，并对观点进行质疑、假设、理论推论、阐述和论证。还能对观点或者事件进行评判、预设、假定、论点、论据、结论等。文秋芳教授还提出五项标准，即清晰性、相关性、逻辑性、深刻性、灵活性。从情感特质方面来讲，好奇、开放、自信、正直、坚毅是国家提倡的五个人格特质。（层级理论模型如图2-1所示）

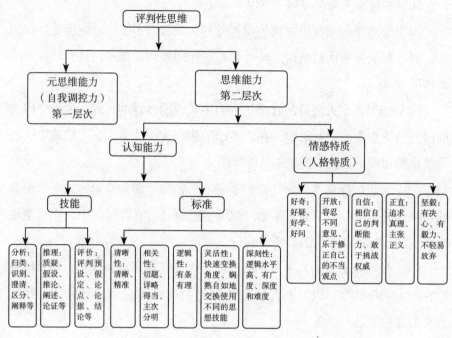

图2-1　文秋芳评判性思维层级理论

2. 布卢姆的教育目标分类法

1956年美国教育心理学家本杰明·塞缪尔·布卢姆提出了认知领域教育目标的分类法。布卢姆将认知领域的目标分为识记、理解、运用、分析、综合和评价六个层次。知道（知识）（knowledge）是指认识并记忆。这一层次所涉及的是具体知识或抽象知识的辨认，用一种非常接近于学生当初遇到的某种观念和现象时的形式，回想起这种观念或现象。理解（comprehension）是指对事物的领会，但不要求深刻的领会，而是初步的，可能是肤浅的。其包括转化、解释、推断等。应用（application）是指对所学习的概念、法则、原理的运用。它要求在没有说明问题解决模式的情况下，学会正确地把抽象概念运用于适当的情况。这里所说的应用是初步的直接应用，而不是全面地、综合地运用知识。分析（analysis）是指把材料分解成它的组成要素部分，从而使各概念间的相互关系更加明确，材料的组织结构更为清晰，详细地阐明基础理论和基本原理。综合

（synthesis）是以分析为基础，全面加工已分解的各要素，并再次把它们按要求重新地组合成整体，以便综合地、创造性地解决问题。它涉及具有特色的表达，制定合理的计划和可实施的步骤，根据基本材料推出某种规律等活动。它强调特性与首创性，是高层次的要求。评价（evaluation）是认知领域里教育目标的最高层次。这个层次的要求不是凭借直观的感受或观察的现象作出评判，而是理性地、深刻地对事物本质的价值作出有说服力的判断，它综合内在与外在的资料、信息，作出符合客观事实的推断。

1994年，安德森（L.W.Anderson）和克拉斯沃尔（D.R.Krathwohl）组织了一大批知名学者，对布卢姆教育目标分类学进行了评判性分析，总结了布卢姆教育目标分类学对教育理论与实践所做出的贡献，同时指出了其不足之处。2001年，安德森等一批教育家对布卢姆教育目标分类学的修订版出版。安德森认知目标分类框架在指导教师教学这方面较之原版布卢姆教育目标分类学有了很大的改善。很好地解决了教学中应该"教什么""怎么教学"以及"为什么这样教学"这三个重要问题，并且在教师的具体教学过程中也给予指导。该书的出版标志着教育目标分类学随着教育领域研究的深入也随之不断发展。安德森认知目标分类框架较之布卢姆原版目标分类学最大的变化就是将认知领域重新划分成知识和认知过程两个维度，在处理知识与能力的关系上安德森版超越了原版。在认知过程维度，是旨在帮助教师明确学生目前掌握和应用知识所能达到的程度。与布卢姆原版相比，首先安德森版目标分类学的认知过程维度仍维持原有的六种水平，但是将原版中的认知水平中的"知识"改为"记忆"，保留了"理解""应用""分析""评价"这几个层次，增加了"创造"作为最高认知层次。这六种类型中，前三类是属于初级层次的认知思维（LOT）问题，而后三类属于高级认知（HOT）思维问题。"记忆"水平是与保持最密切相关的，其余五类认知过程则有助于促进学习迁移。安德森认知目标分类框架中的认知过程维度很好地概括了学生学习活动的表现方式，也有利于帮助教师掌握和拓宽促进迁移的其他几类目标，使之能帮助教师制定和评估旨在促进迁移的目标，而非仅停留在促进保持这类低层次认知过程上。其次还增加了知识维度，知识维度指对知识的分类，用来帮助教师区分什么知识是要教的。两个版本的教育目标分类对比如图2-2所示，修订后的教育目标如图2-3所示。

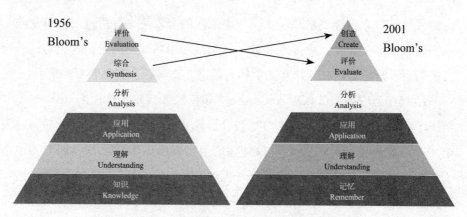

图2-2　布卢姆教育目标分类法修订前后对比图

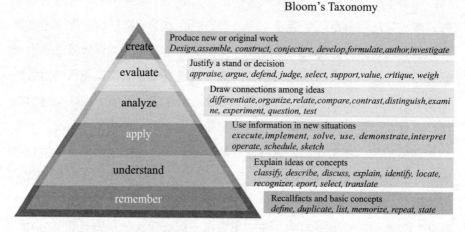

图2-3　修订后的布卢姆教育目标分类法

我们发现，分析、评估和创造这三类高级认知思维和王蕾老师提出的"通过分析、概括、比较、评价、创新等思维活动，在分析问题和解决问题的过程中发展思维品质"是相吻合的。与此同时，我们还发现评判性思维能力在文秋芳教授的层级理论模型中界定为高层次思维能力，主要集中于分析、推理、评价、阐释等方面；在布卢姆目标分类法中属于高级认知思维中的分析和评价。

3. 图式理论

图式理论是本课题依据的另一理论。Cook（1997）将"图式"定义为一个典型实例的心理表征，它有助于人们更快地理解世界，因为"人们通过激活大脑中的相关图式来理解新经历"。因此，根据该理论，英语学习者首先通过听力或阅读输入足够的语言数据；然后寻找可以解释数据的图式。当可以解释数据的图式被发现时，理解就产生了；最后，通过写或说的方式输出数据。因此，读者理解语言材料的过程是读者心理图式与阅读材料所提供的信息相结合的过程。当读者能将心中的图式与信息联系起来，就能获得要传达的意义，从而达到整合的目的。在英语教学中，我们通过阅读来拓展学习者心中的图式，使信息输入与作者的图式形成双向互动。

Bartlett（1932）将图式分为三种类型：语言图式，包括词汇知识、语法知识和衔接知识；内容图式，指的是文本内容区域的背景知识；文本类型的修辞知识和体裁知识层面上的形式图式。

然而，在实际的英语阅读教学中，我们发现学习者不仅困惑对语言图式的匮乏，更是缺乏内容图式和形式图式。因此，笔者认为图式理论可以作为研究的理论基础，通过教学实践帮助学生不仅形成主题意义的语言图式、内容图式，还要逐渐形成不同体裁文本的形式图式。

三、研究设计

我们先查找文献，进行前期调查，了解学生对阅读拓展的态度，确定研究内容和目标，然后和研究成员进行讨论，确定实施方案，在实验班级执行，进行数据分析，并随时根据具体情况进行调整，最后总结出研究结果，写成论文、教案和报告。技术路线如图2-4所示。

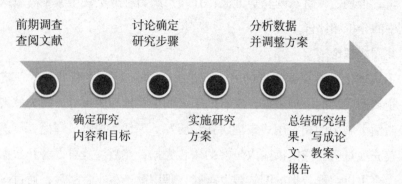

前期调查
查阅文献

讨论确定
研究步骤

分析数据
并调整方案

确定研究
内容和目标

实施研究
方案

总结研究结
果，写成论
文、教案、
报告

图2-4　研究技术路线图

本研究主要采用文献收集、研究—了解学生学情—制订实施方案—实施方案—调整方案—再实施方案—总结研究的流程进行。

技术路线确定后，本着便捷、易实践的原则，课题组根据研究成员所任教年级的分布，确定了研究对象、教学所用的阅读文本等。

（一）研究对象

由于研究人员主要任教我校七、八年级，所以为了研究的便捷性，我们确定了本研究的研究对象为七年级167名学生和八年级105名学生，均属于自然班级，学生的英语起始水平比较薄弱。

（二）阅读教学材料

本研究使用的阅读材料基本都是选自目前我们使用的上海教育牛津版（简称沪教牛津版）七至九年级教材，一是因为教材的阅读材料难度适合我们的研究对象，而且使用方便；二是因为教材的话题贴近学生的生活，学生对此不陌生，容易激活背景知识。

（三）实验过程

实验分别在七、八年级进行，并与全区同年级学生英语成绩做对比分析。研究人员在所任教的坪山同心外国语学校七、八年级的阅读教学中采用评判性阅读的方式。实验过程以行动研究法为主，同时辅之以文献法、比较法、调查法等其他科研方法进行课题研究。实验过程共分两个阶段：第一阶段的实践研究，课题组成员以所教年级的教材顺序开展评判性阅读课的实施，形式以自行设计—反思—研讨—优化为主。本阶段结束后，课题组成员通过问卷调查、访谈、测试等形式发现研究过程中出现的问题后，及时调整研究方案，进行第二阶段的实践研究。在第二阶段的实践研究中，课题组成员主要在设计教学活动之前，进行了文本分析，优化了教学目标和教学活动的设计。

在第二阶段的实践研究中，研究人员主要采用集体研讨，语篇解读—教学设计—提出疑问—优化设计—课堂实践—集体研讨—优化设计—课堂实践—反思—优化设计的方式。这个过程提高了教师的教研能力、语篇研读的能力，同时也形成了不同体裁的文章的评判性阅读教学的流程，使得教师尤其是青年教师在设计教学时有了依据。

最后，实验结束后，课题组组织问卷调查、访谈、测试等方式对实践效果进行检测与验证，经过分析形成研究报告。

（四）检测工具

1. 问卷调查

为了回答第一个研究问题"阅读教学设计的优化是否能促进学生评判思维的发展，不同水平学生表现如何"，课题组成员在实验前、实验中、实验后分别对研究对象进行了问卷调查。为了问卷的有效性和规范性，本研究大部分采用了加利福尼亚评判性思维倾向问卷的内容，而且为了比较研究结果和发现变化，研究人员在研究前后使用了相同的问卷（见附录一）。

2. 前测、中测和后测

研究对象均参加了前测、中测和后测，为了保证测试的效度和信度，本研究所使用的测试题均来自坪山区期末统一测试题中的阅读部分。我们通过SPSS软件对前、中、后测成绩进行比较，确定阅读教学设计的优化是否有助于提高学生的阅读能力。

3. 访谈

为了对第一个研究问题提供补充说明和佐证，我们研究人员在研究对象中抽取了三个层次共18名学生进行了访谈，了解学生研究实施前后在阅读兴趣、评判性思维问题的理解等方面有哪些收获。研究人员把声音转换成了文字，同时，对参与研究的教师也进行了访谈。（访谈问题见附录三）

4. 研讨与反思

研究人员通过自行设计、课堂实践、共同研讨、优化设计、再实践和反思六个环节，试图找到最佳教学设计，在阅读课堂教学中促进学生评判性思维的发展。

第三章　培养学生评判性思维的实践研究

本研究持续两年多的时间，其间进行两轮的教学实践。研究准备阶段，每周二、周五课题组成员共同研讨学习，其间阅读大量的理论与实践文献，确定研究问题、目标和初步实施方案。同时，课题组成员研究制作调查问卷和确定访谈问题，并对研究对象进行了相关调查和访谈，了解学生和教师的需求与疑惑。第一学期结束，研究对象参加了全区统测，本次测试的阅读部分成绩作为前测成绩。

本研究主要采用行动研究法，因此研究实施阶段有两部分：第一阶段实施之后，根据问卷调查、访谈、教师反思等发现的问题，课题组调整方案再进行第二阶段的实践研究。具体研究流程如图3-1所示。

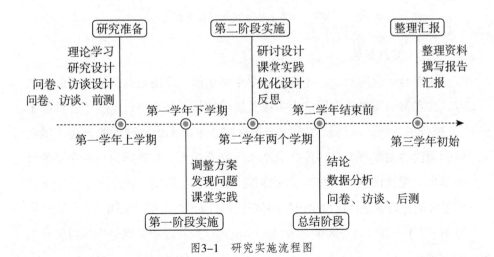

图3-1　研究实施流程图

一、第一阶段实践

（一）实践流程

七、八年级新学期开始，课题组成员开始实施研究，即在阅读教学中注重培养学生的评判性思维能力。本阶段，主要采取的实践方式是教师独自备课设计教学、然后进行课堂实践，实践的过程中遇到问题，在每周的课题组研讨时间进行研讨，优化教学设计，再实践，反思。另外，课题组每位成员在本阶段都进行了课题组内的公开课展示，课题组成员对公开课提出修改意见。如图3-2所示。

图3-2 第一阶段教学实践流程图

（二）实践效果

在参与研究的七、八年级学生学年结束前，课题组对其进行了问卷调查、并在参与实验的两届学生中按英语成绩从"好、中、差"中各抽取了3人进行了访谈，从访谈结果中分析这些学生对英语阅读课的兴趣、最喜欢的阅读活动环节及对评价性活动和问题的观点。对教师的访谈主要侧重于学生对阅读课的喜欢程度、阅读课的教学目标设定、阅读课中学生评判性思维能力培养是否在教学设计中体现等方面（具体见附录四）。研究对象参加了7月初举行的全区期末考试，本次测试的阅读理解部分作为课题研究的中测。

1. 访谈结果

通过对学生前期和中期访谈结果进行对比，发现有以下几个方面的变化。

（1）学生对英语阅读课的兴趣在整体上有了提高，因为阅读课不再是枯燥地讲解课文知识和阅读技巧，而是变成了彼此的分享和讨论。

（2）在阅读环节，多数学生对导入、角色扮演环节尤其是讨论环节比较感兴趣，他们觉得讨论可以激发他们的思考、使思维得到碰撞，能够从多个角度理解事物、了解世界。

（3）学生对评价性的问题了解更加深入，学生认为这样的问题可以让他们深入挖掘文本的背景、人物、情节、主旨，在教师的引导下，他们会在文中或生活中找到细节、例子去支撑他的观点，有理有据地论述自己的观点，从而使他的思维更加开阔，更具有思辨性和逻辑性。

通过对教师前期和中期访谈结果对比，发现有以下几个方面的变化：

（1）实验前，教师对评判性阅读概念比较模糊。实验后，每位教师对于评判性思维能力都有自己不同的见解，并开始付诸实践。

（2）对阅读课的教学目标的转变，从单纯地追求语言知识点的理解和阅读技能的培养到探究作者的写作态度、挖掘写作意图以及阐述对人物或者事件的个人观点与分享。

（3）教师能从课堂活动的多样化到深入研读文本，有意识地培养学生的思辨能力、设计促进评判性思维发展的问题和活动，让学生进行讨论、争辩，以此培养他们敢于表达个人观点的习惯，并形成自己论证的思维方式。

2. 成绩对比

研究人员用统计工具SPSS对学生两次成绩进行了成对样本T检验（表3-1、表3-2）。

表3-1 七年级成对样本检验

项目		成对差分					t	df	Sig.（2-tailed）
		均值	标准差	标准误	差分的95%置信区间				
					下限	上限			
Pair 1	七年级前测至七年级中测	-2.720	2.782	0.197	-3.108	-2.332	-13.826	199	0.000

七年级对比结果显示：中测均分（16.755）高于前测均分（14.035），且P=0.00<0.05.

说明前测、中测成绩在0.05水平上呈显著性差异，即阅读成绩有显著提高，说明阅读课中评判性能力的培养对学生阅读能力有显著的促进作用。

表3-2 八年级成对样本检验

项目		成对差分					t	df	Sig.（2-tailed）
		均值	标准差	均值的标准误	差分的95%置信区间				
					下限	上限			
Pair 1	八年级前测—八年级中测	0.629	6.880	0.592	-0.542	1.801	-13.653	98	0.290

八年级对比结果显示：中测均分（45.385）稍高于前测均分（44.755），P=0.29>0.05.

说明前测、中测成绩在0.05水平上差异不明显，即阅读成绩略有提高，说明阅读课中评判性思维能力的培养对学生阅读能力没有显著的促进作用。

3. 评判性思维倾向性问卷调查结果

七、八年级实验问卷结果如图3-3所示，寻找真理维度和开放思想调查结果如图3-4所示，分析能力和思维的自信心调查结果如图3-5所示，求知欲和认知成熟度调查结果如图3-6所示。

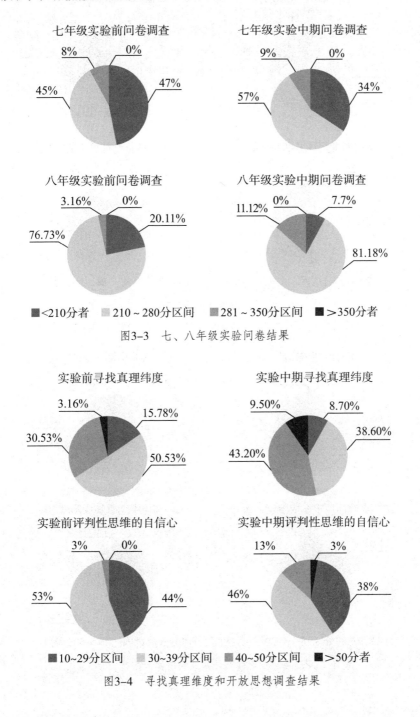

七年级实验前问卷调查

七年级实验中期问卷调查

八年级实验前问卷调查

八年级实验中期问卷调查

■<210分者　　210~280分区间　　281~350分区间　　■>350分者

图3-3　七、八年级实验问卷结果

实验前寻找真理纬度

实验中期寻找真理纬度

实验前评判性思维的自信心

实验中期评判性思维的自信心

■10~29分区间　　30~39分区间　　40~50分区间　　■>50分者

图3-4　寻找真理维度和开放思想调查结果

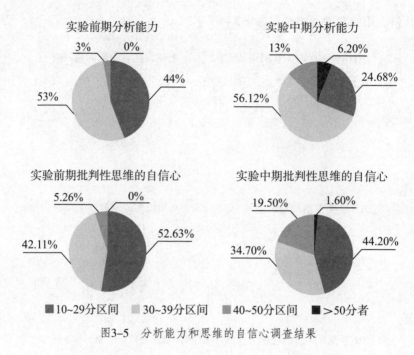

図3-5　分析能力和思維的自信心調査結果

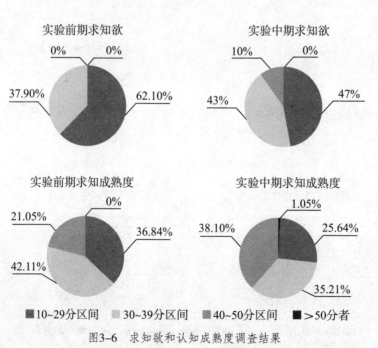

図3-6　求知欲和認知成熟度調査結果

对比结果，可得出以下几点结论。

（1）实验中期七年级学生评判性思维有显著提高。210分以下的学生减少了13%，210~280分的学生由45%上升到57%，281~350分的学生增加了1%，尽管350分以上的学生依然为0%，但学生的思维习惯与评判能力从严重对立到处于矛盾范围，说明评判性思维的倾向向更高发展。

（2）学生实验中期寻找真理、开放思想、分析能力三个维度得分30~39分明显减少，40~50分显著增加，表现出了由矛盾性到评判能力显著增强的趋势。

（3）评判性思维的自信心方面，实验中期40~50分得分区间达到13%，较实验前有显著提高，求知欲方面也表现出了增强的趋势。

（三）存在问题

八年级学生成绩分析中发现仅有40%的学生的阅读成绩有显著提高，还有30%的学生成绩有不同程度的下降。一个可能的原因在于：在课题开始之前教师更关注的是阅读技巧方面的训练，而开始进行课题研究后，教师更关注的是对文本本身的挖掘。技巧的训练短期内是有效果的，而思维的训练在应试测试中短期内效果不显著；另一个原因在于：青春期学生生理与心理发生巨大变化，尤其是情绪的不稳定性导致成绩有所下降。

教师访谈结果反映出教师自身对于评判性思维能力的理解还有待提高，还不清楚具体在哪些环节可以开展促进评判性思维能力发展的活动，只重点在读后环节开展，但又觉得开展得不顺利。

第一轮教学实践中，除了两周一次公开课活动，还进行了两轮阅读专题的同课异构活动，并就阅读课中培养学生评判性思维的设计活动进行评价与反思，发现课堂教学实践中存在以下问题。

1. 教学目标模糊、不可检测，评判性思维的培养目标不显著

例1：沪教牛津版七年级下模块2 Unit 4 Reading：Trees in our daily lives的设计中，教师列出了以下5个学习目标。

（1）Use predicting, scanning, skimming ect. to learn the topic of the article.

（2）Use stratigies like scanning, skimming to get the structure of the article, learn that trees are important to reduce air pollution and important in our daily lives.

（3）Scan the article to find the specific use of trees and find out the language.

（4）Analyze and evaluate the influence of trees on human beings and talk about how trees are important in animals, plants and people's production.

（5）Describe what the world will be like without trees:if forests were destroyed, what results will human beings face.

以上的教学目标，看似让学生使用了predicting，scanning，skimming 等多个阅读策略，但实际上，教师对几个策略的使用目的也是混乱的，比如第一个教学目标，是获取文章主题，我们通常使用的策略是skimming，让学生通过跳读，读文章的题目、段落首尾句，概括出主题，但这里教师罗列了三个功能不同的策略。教师一提出指令，学生面面相觑，无从下手，也就只能逐句读文章。这样既不能训练学生的阅读技能，又会导致学生思维混乱。又比如第二个教学目标是了解树木在减少空气污染和在我们日常生活中的重要性，也是阅读策略的罗列。"了解"这个词是模棱两可的，无法检测的。而实际中，教师带着学生一起画思维导图梳理文章结构，教师边展示课件，边让学生去找，整个过程中学生不需要思考，只需要跟着教师的思路说出来就好了，学生没有思考空间，更不用说评判性思维的发展了。

例2：沪教牛津版八年级上Unit 4 Reading：Great Inventions一课中，教师设计了以下4个学习目标。

（1）Scan the article to get the structure: Time, inventor, process, influence.

（2）Get the information of wheels, telephone and lights, and compare the importance.

（3）Use the sentences describing the development of the inventions to express your ideas.

（4）Imitate the article to introduce other inventions.

按照布卢姆教育目标分类，以上4个教学目标中，第一个是获取文章结构信息，第二个是获取三项发明的具体信息，均属于记忆、理解类；第三个目标是用文章中的语言来表达观点，最后一个目标是模仿文章来介绍一项发明。后面这两个教学目标属于应用类。记忆、理解、应用类是低阶思维，是分析、评价和创造三个高阶思维的基石，不可缺失。但如果阅读教学仅停留在低阶思维阶段，学生的评判性思维能力就很难得到发展。

2. 教师的活动设计没有延续性，不利于评判性思维的形成

由于对评判性思维理解不够深入，教师在设计教学活动时只知道评判性思维包含的内容，比如推测、分析、评价等，但对于在实际教学活动中如何实现这一目标还比较模糊，正所谓只知其一不知其二，所以就达不到想要的效果。

例3：沪教牛津版七年级下Unit 3 Reading：A blind man and his "eyes" in a fire是一篇小故事，详细记述了一位盲人及其导盲犬在宾馆的突发火灾中互助逃生的故事，传达了"动物是人类的好朋友"这一主题。教师在Pre-reading活动中设计了一个根据文章题目、简介部分和图片进行推测故事内容的活动。

T: Now please skim the title, the introduction part and the pictures to predict what may happen in the story and what about the ending.

S1: The dog saved the blind man in a fire.

S2: The dog was the blind man's eyes.

T: Very good.

这个活动就此结束！教师紧接着进行了下个活动。预测活动是激活学生原有阅读图式的非常好的一种形式，但是接下来教师并没有设计检测预测是否合理的任何活动，学生的原有图式被激活了，但如果没有对已激活的图式进行检测和评价的话，他们就无法形成新的阅读图式，评判性思维能力中的自我调控能力无法得到发展。

本节课的主要环节如下。

Ⅰ. Pre-reading

1. Brainstorming: Students brainstorm how guide dogs help the blind in real life.

2. Predicting: Students skim the title, the introduction part and the pictures to make predictions and answer the following questions.

Ⅱ. While-reading

1. Reading for the elements of the story:

Students carefully read the story and fill in the table to find out the necessary elements of stories.

表3-3　A blind man and his "eyes" in a fire

Time		
Place		
Main characters		
The main plots of the story	Beginning	
	Development	
	Ending	

2. Reading for detailed information:

Read and find out how Charlie helped John out of danger.

3. Reading for evaluation and inference:

Students discuss about the following questions:

a. What do you think of John and Charlie?

b. Why wouldn't John go without Charlie?

c. Why did the author write the story?

Ⅲ. Post-reading

1. Role-play: Students act the last two paragraphs out:

2. Discussion: Discuss the following questions in groups.

a. Did John save Charlie or did Charlie save John in the fire? Why?

b. What should we do if we get caught in a fire according to what you learnt from this story?

c. How should human beings get along with animals?（Present a picture in which a man with gun is confronting a bear.）

如果教师对学生的预测结果不加以评价，而是留有悬念，并引导他们进入快速阅读并理清故事脉络，然后把他们的推测结果和故事脉络进行对比，学生就会通过对比读前和读后的阅读图式，形成新的图式。

3. 活动设计脱离文本，偏离了培养评判性思维的目标

教师在教学实践中会有意识地设计一些培养学生评判性思维的活动，如画思维导图、推理、讨论等，但有时会忽略活动与文本内容的关系，导致评判性思维的发展没有支撑点。

例4：沪教牛津版九年级下Unit 3 Reading：The world is in danger，教师在最后一个教学环节，设计了一个小组讨论的环节：

Watch a short video clip to find out what else we can do to protect the Earth and think about what else people can do to save the Earth out of danger.

这个活动是让学生看一个视频并找出保护地球的方法，思考人们还能做哪些。视频的主题是和文本一致的，都是保护地球，但是并没有从文本出发，拓展学生思维，发展他们的评判性思维，而是简单地重复了内容，也就是说，学生即使不读文本，也能根据这个视频去回答问题。这个看似培养评判性思维的活动设计，实际上是文本出现的另一种形式，还是属于学习理解类的范畴，是一种对视频内容的学习理解。

因为文章的四个部分分别描述了温室效应、滥伐森林、人类的坏习惯、一些保护环境的具体做法。那么，教师在设计活动时，如果把文本内容作为铺垫，然后设计分析、判断类的活动，就能更好地促进评判性思维的发展。可以设计一个小组讨论与分享的活动，讨论问题如下。

（1）Do you agree with the writer's opinion that we can make a difference if we change our lifestyle? Why?

（2）As teenagers, what can you do to protect the environment？

这样，学生可以把前面所读内容和自己的生活实践结合起来，进行综合评价，再列出自己的理由，就比较合情合理。

4. 固定框架，限制了学生的思维空间

例5：沪教牛津版八年级上Unit 5 Reading: An exchange visit is educational and interesting一课的执教中，教师向学生解释了题目之后，便带着学生边读边在PPT上展出交换生活动内容的思维导图。

T: What is the title of the article?

S: An exchange visit is educational and interesting.

T: Okay. What is the meaning of "exchange"?

S: 交换!

T: Great! Now please read the article and finish the mind-map（见图3-7）.

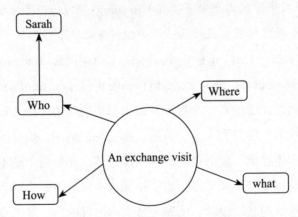

图3-7　The mind-map of an exchange visit

T: Now read the introduction and tell me who is taking part in the program?

S: Students from England. /Sarah, Eric.

T: Right. What are they doing? And where are they now?

S: They are visiting Xinhua Junior High School on an educational exchange. They are in Beijing.

T: Nice. Now let's read the article.

接下来又带着学生一问一答地阅读文章，学生既没有静下来阅读的时间，也没有思考的空间，这个阅读的活动完全由教师主导，学生思维被教师牵着走，处于被动状态。

在阅读活动中运用思维导图梳理、分析，能很好地帮助学生理解、阐释文章内容。但是，如果教师一直带着学生画，就限制了学生的思维发展。教师可以做一个引导者，引导学生了解文章体裁，然后由学生自主完成，通过课堂展示、同伴评价、教师评价的方式，让他们理清文章脉络，再进行深入分析与评价，进而学会自我调控，会更加有效。

5. 活动花样多，导致学生的评判性思维发展没有连续性

教师在设计阅读活动时，为了追求活动的多样性，就分段处理篇章，而且刻意设计不同的活动来检测学生对文本理解的程度。实际上，这种设计恰恰打乱了学生的思维发展，使思维没有连续性，不能层层递进。

例6：沪教牛津版八年级下Unit 3 Reading：Fishing with birds 是一篇说明文，介绍了鸬鹚捕鱼这项中国劳动人民传承千年的古老技艺。文章先简要介绍了渔民王大民的情况及鸬鹚，又细致描写了王大民用鸬鹚捕鱼的具体过程，在最后简述了鸬鹚捕鱼的现状，点明了这一传统技艺面临后继无人的局面。

教师在读中环节设计了下面的活动。

Ⅰ. Reading for main idea

Students scan the first sentence of each paragraph and match each paragraph with their main ideas.

Para. 1 describes a kind of bird.

Para. 2 is about the future of fishing with birds.

Para. 3 describes a fisherman.

Para. 4 describes how the fisherman works.

II. Reading for details

1. Read para 1 and answer the following questions.

A.What is Wang's job?

B. How old is Wang?

C. What's Wang's health condition?

2. Students read para 2 and answer the following questions.

A. What do cormorants look like?

B. What can cormorants do well in?

C. What's special about cormorants?

III. Students read para 3 and fill in the blanks

Time to set off:

First, Wang Damin _____ to stop them from eating big fish.

Then, after his boatin the river, he _____ and use several ways to_____ .

During the day, _____.

After dark, _____.

Finally, the cormorants _____ . Damin _____ into the basket.

IV. Students read para. 4 and answer the following questions

A. What was the past of cormorant fishing?

B.What is the present of cormorant fishing?

C. What might be the future of cormorant fishing?

以上总共有四个大的阅读活动，其中第一个为获取主旨大意的活动，策略指导到位，但获取细节信息的活动（II、III、IV）比较凌乱，花样比较多：回答问题、句子填空等。看似把整篇文章分段落设计任务让学生读的做法降低了学生阅读的难度，但实际上这种处理方式会导致学生不能从整体的角度理解文本，使理解碎片化，而且他们没有充足的时间理解、感悟作者的意图，而是疲于完成教师花样繁多的任务。另一个问题就是，教师在读中活动中没有设计促进学生评判性思维发展的问题，如 Why are few young people interested in fishing with birds?

6. 教师缺少体裁分析意识，对评判性思维培养的活动设计没有清晰的界限

本研究使用的沪教牛津版初中英语教材，涵盖了记叙、说明、故事小说和论述四类体裁的文章，尽管课题组成员在实践前已经达成共识：要有体裁意识，按体裁设计评判性思维培养的教学活动，但有些教师设计教学活动时，依然缺少体裁意识，没有根据不同体裁文章的不同特点分析文本，对于不同体裁文本的评判性思维活动的设计混淆不清。

例7：上教牛津版九上Unit 1 Reading：Archimedes and the gold crown是一篇讲述名人逸闻趣事的故事。

教师在读前环节用了教材本身配套的背景知识小测验部分。

1. Which of these ancient countries is in Europe?

　　A. Greece　　　　　　　　　B. Egypt

2. Which of these people lived in ancient Greece?

　　A. Archimedes　　　　　　　B. Julius Caesar

3. What was Archimedes?

　　A. A scientist.　　　　　　　B. A painter.

4. Archimedes died in 212 BC. How long ago was that?

　　A. About 1,800 years ago.　　B. About 2,200 years ago.

这个环节旨在激发学生的背景知识，为故事阅读做一些铺垫，是可行的。教师在读中环节，设计了以下的活动。

Activity 1: Read and put the pictures into the right order.

图3-8   Diagrammatic sketch

Activity 2: Read and answer the following questions.

1. Who was the crown probably made for?

2. What was Archimedes doing in the first picture?

3. Why was Archimedes so excited ?

4. What is in the right pot in the second picture?

5. What happened when Archimedes got into the bath?

6. What did the crown maker do to the crown?

在读后活动中，教师设计了故事复述和讨论两个活动。

教师在文本分析时对文本体裁进行分析是为了解其语言特征，文体的语篇结构等。在阅读教学中，教师需要通过体裁分析了解英语阅读文章的交际目的，且掌握英语阅读文本的语言特点以及要对语篇内容进行更深层次的分析与概括，这样才能更好地设计教学活动，更清晰地分辨哪些环节可以培养学生的评判性思维。通过对这篇故事的文本分析，我们知道文章的体裁是故事类体裁，讲述了阿基米德接到国王要求他甄别真假皇冠的命令后，百思不得其解之时，竟然在自己洗澡的过程中，想到了鉴别方法，帮助国王揭露了造冠者的阴谋。作者通过描述阿基米德测试"真假王冠"，告诉我们遇到问题要敢于尝试，不断探索，从生活中找方法，培养自己热爱科学的意识。整篇故事以清晰的时间、地点、人物为线索。文章共9段，分3个部分。第一部分（1～5段）描述了阿基米德接到国王任务——测试王冠真假后的苦恼和尝试。第二部分（6～8段）讲述了阿基米德测试王冠真假的过程。第三部分（9段）讲述了国王得知假王冠后，对造冠者所做的处罚。

针对这一类的体裁，教师要引导学生通过故事六要素"who，where，when，what，how，why"梳理文章脉络，然后再进行故事情节的分析，即开端、发展、转折、结局等，如图3-9所示。

图3-9　文章脉络示意图

a. The problem was difficult to solve.

b. The king sent the crown maker to the prison.

c. He proved the crown was not completely made of gold.

d. The king sent the crown to Archimedes to find out if it was completely made of gold.

e. Archimedes thought up an idea when he was taking a bath.

第一次接触故事类阅读，教师可以列出一些句子，让学生根据情节发展完成故事发展线索图。经过几篇阅读之后，教师可以让学生分小组完成，再分享、互评，帮助学生评判性思维的发展。

二、第二阶段实践

一个学期的实践结束后，我们针对第一轮实践中取得的一些成果和发现的问题，继续查证文献，研讨解决问题的方案，并通过不断实践优化教学设计。在接下来的一个学年里，我们多次研讨，并进行多次公开课，同课异构，课程反思，论文撰写等活动，旨在了解经过36周的研究实践之后，学生对阅读课及阅读课中的活动尤其是分析、推理、评价性活动的理解有没有发生变化；学生的评判性思维能力有没有提高；课题组教师评判性思维阅读课堂教学有没有得到改善或提升。

（一）教学实践方式的优化

本阶段，主要采取的实践方式是教师独自进行语篇解读、教学设计、同年级研究研讨教师的教学设计并提出质疑与建议、优化教学设计、课堂实践、全体研讨、课堂再实践、教学设计定稿、教学反思。在长达两个学期的实践中，课题组形成了整体教学改进方法和程序，如图3-10所示。

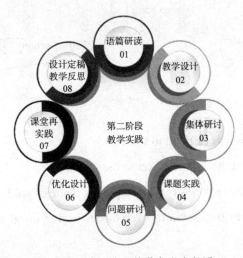

图3-10　第二阶段教学实践流程图

（二）教学设计的优化策略

1.教学前要进行文本解读

教师在设计教学活动前，须从what，why，how三个维度进行文本解读。

　　文本解读是落实活动观、实现学科育人的逻辑起点（王蔷，2018）。教师解读文本时，从what，why，how三个维度，充分挖掘文本的主要内容、结构、语言、修辞和作者意图。教师文本解读的水平决定了教学活动设计的合理性，只有把文本解读到位了，才能设计可检测的教学目标，也才能设计出培养评判性思维的活动。例1和例2的教学目标的问题，就是因为教师没有充分阅读文本，没有从三个维度对文本进行解读而导致的，所以教师至少阅读文本10篇、再从what，why，how三个维度分析文本之后才能设定教学目标。例如，沪教版八上Unit 5 Reading：An exchange visit is educational and interesting！通过文本解读后，可以设定以下教学目标。

　　在本节课学习结束时，学生能够：

　　（1）根据标题、引言和图片预测文章内容、结构。

　　（2）通过画思维导图梳理这篇新闻报道的关键信息，如谁、在哪里、干了什么等。

　　（3）分析Sara的情感变化。

　　（4）理解作者让我们尊重不同文化的意图，为来你校的交流生设计一些活动。

　　（5）归纳新闻报道文体的特点，评价这篇报道的优点和缺点。

　　另外，教师通过对文本进行解读，才能从文本出发，发现并设计评判性思维生长点的活动。

　　培养学生的评判性思维需要教师鼓励学生对阅读文本进行审视和质疑，提出自己的想法，通过提供支撑证据，对自己的观点进行合理的解释，这个过程就是评判性思维生长的过程，能设计这些活动的点就是思维的生长点。评判性思维的发展需要语言和内容的支撑，学生的输出也依赖于语言和内容。教师在活动设计时也必须考虑这一点，活动必须能让学生使用到文本中所学的内容和有关语言，其思维才能够得以生长。

　　评判性思维属于高阶思维，高阶思维需要低阶思维——记忆、理解、运用的铺垫，才能逐步发展。学生对作者观点的评价、作者意图的推理都需要在充分理解作者的观点，分析观点和证据是否存在因果关系之后，才能形成自己的判断,这是一个循序渐进的过程。阅读的过程刚好相反,它需要运用自己已有的有关知识来对文本内容进行重建,从而去探索该文本的深层意义,同时,作者会运用各种写作手段,运用不同框架结构来表达自己的想法。这些均构成了思维的生长点,所以教师要善于反复研究、剖析文本,发现和利用这些生长点来设计教学活动。

2. 学习活动的设计要有延续性

读前预测,是培养评判性思维的有效活动,不管是哪一种体裁的文章,教师都可以设计读前让学生根据题目、图片、简介等对文章内容或结构通过头脑风暴等形式进行预测的活动,唤醒学生原有的阅读结构图式,并记录下来。这一环节也培养了学生的作者意识,为读后的写作教学做好了谋篇布局的准备。但教师在读中环节的活动设计中,一定要让学生运用跳读等策略梳理文章结构,然后与学生自己的预测进行对比分析与评价,这就是思维的延续。当然在这个过程中,可以质疑题目的合理性、文章结构布局的优劣等,据此做出优化并形成新的结构图式。

根据这个理念,我们可以把上一章例3的教学活动设计优化为如图3-11所示的流程。

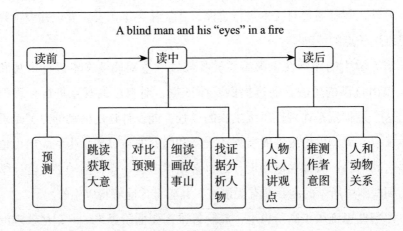

图3-11 教学活动流程

（三）引导学生自己用思维导图的形式梳理文章信息

教师在设计梳理文本内容的活动时，经常使用思维导图或者表格形式，这是很好的活动方式。思维导图的运用能发散学生的思维，有效地激发、丰富和巩固阅读过程中所需要的语言图示、内容图示和形式图示（沈爱芬，2014：12）。

鼓励学生用思维导图梳理文章内容，需要教师先做示范，并对展示的思维导图进行说明，然后让学生独自完成思维导图、小组内分享导图、班级分享、同伴评价导图，以发展评判性思维的分析、评判、自我调控能力。图3-12是两位学生在阅读沪教版八年级上Unit 5 Reading: An exchange visit is educational and interesting 时，所画的思维导图。

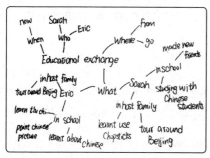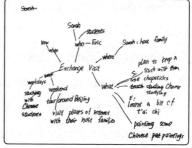

图3-12　学生绘制的思维导图

两位同学都是从故事六要素who，when，where，what，why，how梳理内容，但从思维导图的差异处可以看出他们对文章理解的角度是不同的，差异主要集中在"做了什么"方面。第一位同学按人物分析之后，又按地点不同进行解读；第二位同学按时间（工作日和周末）来梳理他们做的事情。

通过他们在班级分享、讲解思路，同学们又展开了讨论，最终对这一次的交换项目有了深刻的理解。在这个基础之上，教师再设计一个读后问题链，就能更好地促进学生评判性思维的发展了。

（四）用问题链的形式，促进学生评判性思维的发展

问题链是指由问题组合而成的链条。王后雄（2010）认为：问题链就

是教师按照教学目标和教学内容，根据学生已有的知识或经验，针对学生学习过程中可能产生的困惑，将文本内容转换成为层次鲜明、具有系统性的一连串问题。学生通过解决问题链上的问题，将文本信息与大脑中已有的认知图式进行互通，从而实现文本意义建构与发展思维广度和深度的目的。问题链是一种能够关照到教学内容系统性、整体性、关联性、层次性的提问方式。

例8：在沪教牛津版七年级下 Unit 8 Reading：My lifetime hobby—studying stars 一课的学习活动设计中，教师的处理方式如下。

Activity 1: Predicting

T: Guys, please read the title and tell me what information you can get.

S1: His hobby is studying stars.

S2: He likes studying stars all his life because we can see the word "lifetime".

S3: The story is about his hobby.

T: Great! You are so excellent that you have got so much information. If you were the writer, what would you write to tell us your lifetime hobby?

S4: I will introduce when I started my hobby and how it started.

S5: And the hobby.

S6: Why I like it all my life.

Activity 2: Reading and comparing

T: Now please skim the story and get the main idea of each paragraph.

Please compare the main ideas with what you tell me to see who is the better writer.

Activity 3: Read and answer questions

（1）What made Patrick begin to like studying stars?

（2）What did he use to do on clear nights?

（3）What did he think of the stars?

（4）How did he turn his hobby into his career?

（5）Why can his program last so long?

（6）What does the word "lively" mean? How do you know that?

（7）What advice does he give? Do you agree?

这个问题链是基于教师对文本深度解读的基础上，并基于布卢姆的目标分类而设计的。整个问题链有三个层次：（1）~（3）属于认识与理解层次，是对文章内容的基本了解；（4）~（6）是对文章内容的分析、推理层次；（7）属于评价层次。

教师通过设计这样的问题链逐步引导学生在已有知识的基础上建构新知识，养成独立思考的意识和能力，逐步发展创造性思维。当然，教师在设计问题链时注意问题要难易适中，循序渐进，有逻辑性，要让不同层次的学生都能去精心阅读与思考。比如英语水平稍薄弱的学生也可以回答前三个问题，对于后面的四个问题虽然回答不出，或不能完全回答，但他们也会积极地去思考，等水平稍好的同学分享的时候，就能理解一二，也就有了豁然开朗的感觉。

（五）设计学习活动时要有体裁意识，根据不同体裁设计不同的学习活动

Bhatia在教学实践中提出了体裁的认知结构，并且指出特定体裁具有特定的规则，强调体裁结构的特有形式。体裁分析是多维度的文本解析方法，第一，我们运用体裁分析方法形成具体体裁的图式结构。第二，掌握其文本建构的基本原理，用体裁分析理论指导英语阅读教学。人们在进行体裁分析时，主要对所读文本体裁的篇章结构与篇章特点进行解析，并且掌握语篇的形式与结构图式进而逐步建构自身语篇的认知体系（Bhatia，1993）。

例如，本研究所指的记叙文主要包括历史、传记、日记、新闻报道等，也就是说明类记叙文，主要是根据when，where，who，what，why和how六要素来记叙。因此，教师在设计记叙文体裁的文本时，首先就要让学生从六要素入手理清叙述内容。在记叙文中通常有一些与语篇主旨大意高度相关的句子，而这些句子或表达包含深层含义，需要教师引导学生通过上下文推理分析，所以学生只要理解了这些就可以理解作者写作意图和目的。

又如，说明文通常说明某一事物的特征、普遍真理、阐述科学道理和对事物发生、发展、结果等进行介绍、说明的一种文体（王水莲，2001）。说明文主要目的是阐述，解释或探讨各种问题，帮助读者获得必要的信息，说明文一般按总—分、一般—特殊的顺序进行说明，使人们对事物有个清晰、完整的了解和认识。说明文的基本信息主要包括说明对象、说明的事实，理由和观点等。常用的说明方法有举例，分类，比较，下定义，列数字等。 教师对说明文的体裁特征了解得非常清晰的基础上设计的教学活动会使学生更加明晰。

总之，教师在体裁分析的基础上设计学生的学习活动，会让学生逐渐有体裁意识，对于阅读不同体裁的文章，也会形成自己的体裁阅读图式，更有利于对文章的理解。

（六）根据学习目标设计自我评价表，提高学生评判性思维中的自我调控能力

自我评价是学习者对自己学习行为的各个方面的评判，如学习进度、学习时间安排、学习策略的使用、学习效果等。自我评价是自主学习过程中的一个重要环节，也是一种重要的自主学习能力和自主学习策略（庆维国，2003：112，转引自胡明勇，2010）。自我评价在学习活动中起到非常重要的作用，学生可以通过自我评价来检验自己的学习效果，不断修正和改善自己的学习行为，使自己的学习朝着既定的标准和目标靠拢，这也可以促进评判性思维中自我调控能力的发展。学生通过积极的自我评价能增强自我肯定，激励自己更加努力。即使学生在自评中发现自己有很多没有达成的目标，他们也能通过自我评价了解其真实的学习情况，为达成更高目标而加倍努力。

例9：教师在教授沪教牛津版八年级上Unit 2 Reading：The king and the rice时，通过文本解析后，对学习目标设定如下。

（1）根据插图和标题，预测故事的发展。

（2）获取梳理故事的基本要素（时间、地点、人物、事件起因、经过、结尾）。

（3）根据梳理的信息，能扮演国王或者老者的身份复述整个故事。

（4）依据关键信息，分析国王和智者性格和情感变化。

（5）分析作者的写作意图，对故事和人物进行评价。

教师根据所设定的学习目标和内容，给学生设计了自我评价表，如下所示。

Please tick the sentence if you agree.

※ I can predict the story according to the pictures, the introduction and the title.

※ I can find the elements: who, where, when, what, why and how.

※ I can retell the story with my own words.

※ I can tell how the story is developed.

※ I can state my opinions on the characters and give my reasons.

※ I can analyze the changes of feelings of the characters.

※ I can evaluate the story.

以上评价表是对学习目标的检测，学生通过对照自我评价表的选项，可以一目了然地了解本节课学习目标的达成情况，根据达成程度，可以调整自己下节课的学习投入状态，也可以再次对照评价表对文本进行深度阅读和学习。

第四章　培养学生评判性思维能力的数据分析

　　我们研究人员，在第二轮教学实践结束后，对研究对象进行了问卷调查、访谈、测试，为了研究的信度和效度，问卷、访谈内容均和实验前保持了一致。

一、问卷调查结果对比与分析

　　研究人员对研究对象对比分析了实验前后的调查问卷，结果表明较实验前，被试者的评判性思维倾向有明显增强；与评判性思维严重对立者的学生数量明显减少；有1%的学生的评判性思维倾向于全面强。

　　实验前，研究人员对八年级学生分发了105份问卷，收到有效问卷95份。对七年级学生分发了167份问卷，收到有效问卷152份。实验结束后，实验人员再次对研究对象进行问卷调查，分别收到有效问卷97份、154份。为保证实验前后对比有效，本研究对实验前后八年级学生中的有效问卷95份和七年级学生中的有效问卷152份分别进行对比分析。分析标准：处于210~280分区间：表明被试者的评判性思维倾向处于矛盾范围；低于210分者：表明被试者的倾向与评判性思维严重对立；281~350分者：表明有正性评判性思维性格；高于350分者：表明被试者的评判性思维各方面都强。具体分析如下：

七年级学生实验前后问卷调查结果：

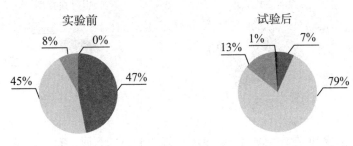

图4-1　七年级学生实验前后调查问卷评判性思维倾向饼状对比图

从对比数据可知，实验后，79%被试者的评判思维倾向处于矛盾范围；13%的被试者有正性评判性思维；7%的被试者与评判思维严重对立；1%的被试者的评判性思维各方面都强。较实验前，有正向评判思维的学生增加了5%；倾向于矛盾的学生增加了34%，明显增多；而与评判性思维严重对立者的学生数量明显减少；有1%的学生的评判性思维各方面都强，这是很大的突破。

以下是细化至评判思维的七个维度，分别是寻找真理、开放思想、分析能力、系统化能力、评判性思维的自信心、求知欲和认知成熟度进行调查。评价标准：10~29分区间者：表明评判性思维倾向较差；30~39分区间者，表明被试者对该倾向持矛盾态度；40~50分区间者，该倾向方面是弱的；＞50分者，表明被试者在评判性思维倾向方面为强。

由图4-2可见，实验前1%的学生在评判性思维的寻找真理方面较强，实验后11%的学生在评判性思维的寻找真理方面较强，实验前16%的学生该方面倾向较弱，实验后44%的学生该方面倾向较弱，实验前53%的学生寻找真理的评判思维倾向持矛盾态度，实验后39%的学生寻找真理的评判思维倾向持矛盾态度。实验前30%的学生该思维倾向较差，实验后6%的学生该思维倾向较差。整体呈上升趋势。

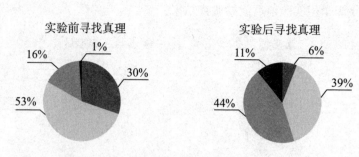

实验前寻找真理　　　　　　　实验后寻找真理

■10~29分区间　■30~39分区间　■40~50分区间　■>50分者

图4-2　七年级学生实验前后评判性思维寻找真理倾向饼状对比图

由图4-3可见，实验前1%的学生具有较强的开放思想，实验后5%的学生具有较强的开放思想。实验前16%的学生该方面倾向较弱，实验后这个数据为52%。实验前46%的学生对自身的开放思想持矛盾态度，实验后这个数据为38%。实验前37%的学生该思维倾向较差，而实验后该数据为5%，人数明显下降，学生整体开放思想程度有所改善。

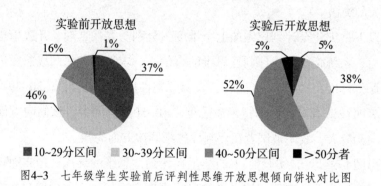

实验前开放思想　　　　　　　实验后开放思想

■10~29分区间　■30~39分区间　■40~50分区间　■>50分者

图4-3　七年级学生实验前后评判性思维开放思想倾向饼状对比图

由图4-4可见，实验前1%的学生具有较强的分析能力，实验后2%的学生具有较强的分析能力。实验前8%的学生分析能力较弱，实验后12%的学生分析能力较弱。实验前43%的学生对分析能力持矛盾态度，实验后66%的学生对分析能力持矛盾态度。实验前48%的学生分析能力较差，实验后20%学生分析能力较差。学生的分析能力有显著提高。

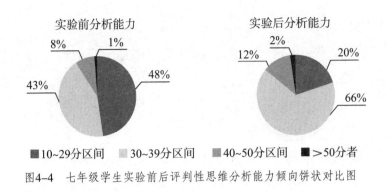

图4-4　七年级学生实验前后评判性思维分析能力倾向饼状对比图

由图4-5可见，实验前1%的学生具有较强的系统化能力，实验后3%的学生具有较强的系统化能力。6%的学生实验前该方面倾向较弱，实验后这个数据变成20%。实验前41%的学生对自身的系统化能力持矛盾态度，实验后这个数据变为66%。实验前52%的学生系统化能力较差，实验后这个数据变为11%。学生的系统化能力整体有所提高。

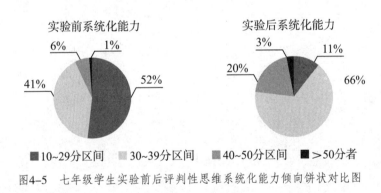

图4-5　七年级学生实验前后评判性思维系统化能力倾向饼状对比图

由图4-6可见，实验前没有学生具有较强的评判性思维的自信心，实验后4%的学生具有较强的评判性思维的自信心。实验前2%的学生该方面倾向较弱，实验后7%的学生该方面倾向较弱。实验前35%的学生对自身的评判性思维的自信心持矛盾态度，实验后55%的学生对自身的评判性思维的自信心持矛盾态度。实验前63%的学生该思维倾向较差，实验后34%的学生该思维倾向较差。学生对评判性思维的自信心有所提高。

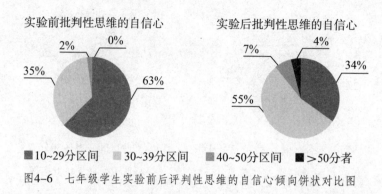

实验前批判性思维的自信心　　　　实验后批判性思维的自信心

2%　0%　　　　　　　7%　4%
35%　　63%　　　　55%　34%

■10~29分区间　■30~39分区间　■40~50分区间　■>50分者

图4-6　七年级学生实验前后评判性思维的自信心倾向饼状对比图

由图4-7可见，实验前没有学生具有较强的求知欲，实验后1%的学生具有较强的求知欲。实验前5%的学生该方面倾向较弱，实验后7%学生该方面倾向较弱。实验前38%的学生对自身的求知欲持矛盾态度，实验后54%学生对自身的求知欲持矛盾态度。实验前57%学生求知欲较差，实验后38%的学生求知欲较差。总体而言，学生的求知欲有整体提升。

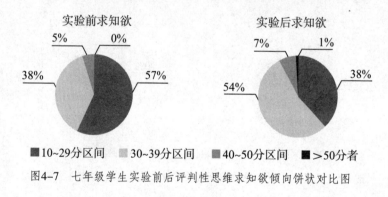

实验前求知欲　　　　　　　实验后求知欲

5%　0%　　　　　　7%　1%
38%　　57%　　　　54%　38%

■10~29分区间　■30~39分区间　■40~50分区间　■>50分者

图4-7　七年级学生实验前后评判性思维求知欲倾向饼状对比图

由图4-8可见，实验前没有学生具有较强的认知成熟度，实验后3%的学生具有较强的认知成熟度。实验前13%的学生该方面倾向较弱，实验后该数据为24%。实验前45%的学生对自身的认知成熟度持矛盾态度，实验后该数据变为37%。实验前42%的学生认知成熟度较差，实验后36%的学生认知成熟度较差。学生的整体认知成熟度有所提高。

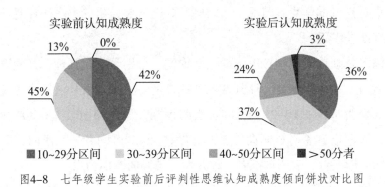

实验前认知成熟度　　　　　实验后认知成熟度

■10~29分区间　■30~39分区间　■40~50分区间　■>50分者

图4-8　七年级学生实验前后评判性思维认知成熟度倾向饼状对比图

综上可知，七年级学生在这七个维度中，实验后超过50分的所占比例分别是寻找真理11%、开放思想5%、分析能力2%、系统化能力3%、评判性思维的自信心4%、求知欲1%、认知成熟度3%。所以，评判性思维能力中求知成熟度是较高的，其他能力所占比例很低。即很少学生在评判性思维的七个维度都表现出较强的能力。大部分学生具有较弱的寻求真理、开放思想和认知成熟度。大部分学生对评判性思维中的分析能力、系统化能力、评判性思维的自信心、求知欲四个维度具有矛盾态度。

八年级学生实验前后问卷调查结果见图4-9。

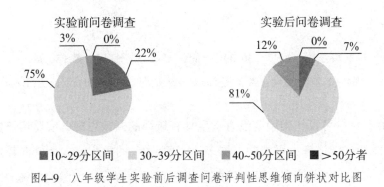

实验前问卷调查　　　　　　实验后问卷调查

■10~29分区间　■30~39分区间　■40~50分区间　■>50分者

图4-9　八年级学生实验前后调查问卷评判性思维倾向饼状对比图

从图4-9所示对比数据可知，实验后，81%的被试者的评判性思维倾向处于矛盾范围；12%的被试者有正性评判性思维；7%的被试者与评判性思维严重对立；0%的被试者的评判性思维各方面都强。较实验前，有正向评判思维的学生增加了9%；倾向于矛盾的学生增加了6%；而与评判性思维严重对立者的学生数量减少了15%。对比结果显示，本次研究对评判性思维有促进作用。

以下是细化至评判性思维的七个维度，分别是寻找真理、开放思想、分析能力、系统化能力、评判性思维的自信心、求知欲和认知成熟度进行调查。评价标准：10~29分区间：表明评判性思维倾向较差；30~39分区间者，表明被试者对该倾向持矛盾态度；40~50区间者，该倾向方面是弱的；50分以上者，表明被试者在评判性思维倾向方面为强。

由图4-10可见，实验后4%的学生在评判性思维的寻找真理方面较强，实验前为3%，稳步提升。实验后42%的学生该方面倾向较弱，实验前为30%，也表现出上升趋势。实验后50%学生寻找真理的评判性思维倾向持矛盾态度，实验前为51%。实验后4%的学生该思维倾向较差，实验前为16%，该群体有显著下降。

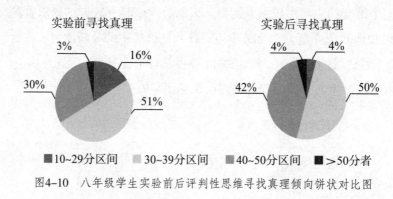

图4-10　八年级学生实验前后评判性思维寻找真理倾向饼状对比图

由图4-11可见，实验前没有学生具有较强的开放思想，实验后该数据是1%，具有较强开放思想的人增多。实验前3%的学生该方面倾向较好，实验后39%的学生该方面倾向较好，比例有显著提升。实验前53%的学生对自身的开放思想持矛盾态度，实验后该数据为50%，人数有所减少。实验前44%的学生该思维倾向较差，实验后该数据为10%，明显减少。

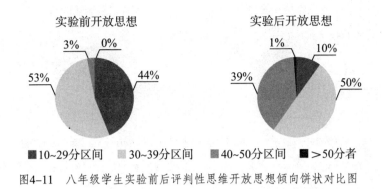

图4-11　八年级学生实验前后评判性思维开放思想倾向饼状对比图

由图4-12可见，实验前有较强的分析能力的学生为零，实验后1%的学生具有较强的分析能力，实验前11%的学生分析能力较强，实验后18%的学生分析能力较强，实验前58%的学生对分析能力持矛盾态度，实验后70%学生对分析能力持矛盾态度，人数明显增加。实验前31%的学生分析能力较差，实验后11%学生分析能力较差，有显著降低。

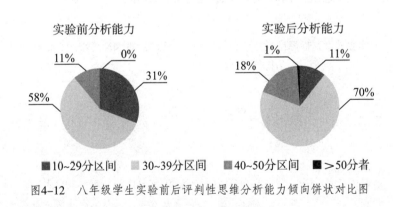

图4-12　八年级学生实验前后评判性思维分析能力倾向饼状对比图

由图4-13可见，实验前没有学生具有较强的系统化能力，实验后1%的学生具有较强的系统化能力，实验前63%的学生对自身的系统化能力持矛盾态度，实验后70%的学生对自身的系统化能力持矛盾态度。实验前23%的学生系统化能力较差，实验后15%学生系统化能力较差。学生的系统化能力呈明显上升趋势。

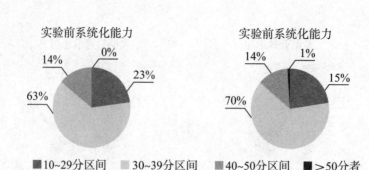

实验前系统化能力　　　　　实验前系统化能力

■10~29分区间　■30~39分区间　■40~50分区间　■>50分者

图4-13　八年级学生实验前后评判性思维系统化能力倾向饼状对比图

由图4-14可见，实验前没有学生有较强的评判性思维的自信心，实验后2%的学生具有较强的评判性思维的自信心。实验前15%的学生评判性思维的自信心倾向较弱，实验后37%的学生自信心较弱。实验前47%的学生对自身的评判性思维的自信心持矛盾态度，实验后52%的学生对自身的评判性思维的自信心持矛盾态度。实验前38%的学生该思维倾向较弱，实验后9%的学生该思维倾向较弱。整体也是上升趋势。

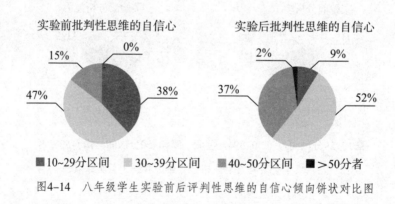

实验前批判性思维的自信心　　　实验后批判性思维的自信心

■10~29分区间　■30~39分区间　■40~50分区间　■>50分者

图4-14　八年级学生实验前后评判性思维的自信心倾向饼状对比图

由图4-15可见，实验前40%的学生求知欲倾向较弱，实验后7%的学生求知欲倾向较弱。实验前52%的学生对自身的求知欲持矛盾态度，实验后70%的学生对自身的求知欲持矛盾态度。实验前7%的学生求知欲较强，而试验后，22%的学生求知欲较强，这部分增加了15%的学生。实验前后求知欲非常强的学生没有发生变化，均为1%。

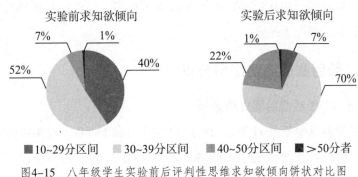

图4-15　八年级学生实验前后评判性思维求知欲倾向饼状对比图

由图4-16的对比数据可见，实验前没有学生具有较强的认知成熟度，实验后1%的学生具有较强的认知成熟度。实验前3%的学生认知成熟度较弱，实验后5%的学生成熟度较弱。实验前41%的学生对自身的认知成熟度持矛盾态度，实验后49%的学生对自身的认知成熟度持矛盾态度。实验前56%的学生认知成熟度较差，实验后45%的学生认知成熟度较差。

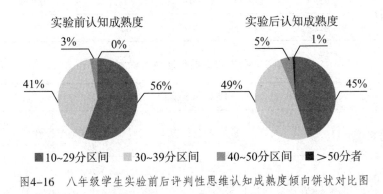

图4-16　八年级学生实验前后评判性思维认知成熟度倾向饼状对比图

综上可知，学生在评判性思维寻找真理、开放思想、分析能力、系统化能力、评判性思维的自信心、求知欲和认知成熟度七个维度上表现都不同。81%的被试者评判性思维倾向处于矛盾范围，12%的被试者有正性评判性思维，7%的被试者与评判思维严重对立。70%的学生在系统化能力、分析能力、求知欲方面表现出矛盾态度。50%的学生在寻找真理、开放思想、评判性思维的自信心、认知成熟度方面表现出矛盾态度。在评判性思维倾向方面较强的学生很少，大部分处于倾向弱和矛盾态度方面，评判性思维倾向较差的学生比例相比前测阶段少了很多。而学生在评判性思维倾向的各个维度都有所提高。

二、前后测成绩对比与分析

（一）SPSS 对前后测成绩分析

下面用数据分析统计工具SPSS17.0对七年级164名、八年级98名均参加了研究前后两次测试的学生的成绩进行了成对样本T检验，以了解阅读教学设计的优化是否能提高学生的阅读能力。

七年级学生前后测数据如表4-1、表4-2所示。

表4-1　2020年毕业生前后测成对样本统计量

成对样本统计量		均值	N	标准差	均值的标准误
对1	前测	37.994	164	12.677	0.989
	后测	42.915	164	7.985	0.624

表4-2　七年级学前后测成对样本检验

成对样本检验								
对1前测（七年级上期末区统考）至后测（八年级下期末区统考）	成对差分					t	df	Sig.（双侧）
	均值	标准差	均值的标准误	差分的95%置信区间		—	—	—
				下限	上限			
	−4.921	14.247	1.112	−7.117	−2.724	−4.423	163	0.000

从两次测试对比中，可以看出后测均分（42.915）高于前测均分（37.994），且P=0.000<0.05. 说明前测、后测成绩在0.05水平上呈显著性差异，即阅读成绩有显著提高，说明阅读课中评判性思维能力的培养显著地提高了学生的阅读能力和水平。

八年级学生前后测数据如表4-3、表4-4所示。

表4-3 2019年毕业生前后测成对样本统计量

成对样本统计量					
		均值	N	标准差	均值的标准误
对1	前测	18.520	98	5.942	0.600
	后测	27.260	98	1.927	0.195

表4-4 八年级学生前后测成对样本检验

成对样本检验								
对1前测（八年级上期末区统考）至后测（九年级下期末区统考）	成对差分					t	df	Sig.（双侧）
	均值	标准差	均值的标准误	差分的95%置信区间		—	—	—
				下限	上限			
	−8.740	6.283	0.635	−9.999	−7.480	−13.770	97	0.000

从两次测试对比中，可以看出后测均分（27.260）高于前测均分（18.520），且$P=0.000<0.05$。说明前测、后测成绩在0.05水平上呈显著性差异，即该研究对象后测阅读成绩与前测阅读成绩相比有显著提高，说明阅读课中评判性思维能力的培养显著地提高了学生的阅读能力和水平。

综合两批研究对象的前后测成绩对比，可以得出以下结论：在初中英语阅读教学中培养学生的评判性思维，对其阅读能力的提高有显著作用。

（二）前后测成绩频次分布分析

除了使用SPSS，研究人员还采用了其他方法来保证研究的信度和效度。因此，对两次测试的得分进行收集，并从频次分布的角度进行分析。（表4-5、表4-6）

表4-5　七年级学生前后测阅读成绩频次分布表

阅读成绩（满分60）	60-51	50-41	40-31	30以下
前测	40	57	53	14
后测	59	64	41	0

表4-6　八年级学生前后测阅读成绩频次分布表

阅读成绩（满分60）	30-26	20-26	20-16	15-11	10以下
前测	18	22	25	21	12
后测	66	32	0	0	0

　　通过对两批研究对象的前测和后测成绩分布比较，我们可以得出高分的学生比研究前的学生更多。低分学生的数量也下降了很多。中分学生的分布也发生了很大变化，更多的高分学生出现了。研究人员还发现，中等水平的学生成绩变化最大，七年级开始参与实验的学生中高水平的学生有进步，但不是很明显，而八年级开始参与实验的学生中高水平学生数量明显增加。低水平的学生成绩也有不同程度的提高，另外，八年级开始参与实验的学生中低水平学生进步非常大，这可能与毕业班的学习氛围和训练强度有关系。

（三）前后测成绩与参照样本对比分析

　　由于某些原因，课题组无法对研究对象与区兄弟学校同水平学生进行独立样本T检验，但为了证明研究的有效性，作者将本校研究对象的前后测均分与区均分进行了比较。（表4-7、表4-8）

表4-7　七年级实验前后成绩与全区对比分析

七年级学科对比分析					区排名
项目	单位	总人数	参加人数	平均分（总分85分）全体	
七年级实验前测（七上）	同心外国语学校	167	163	62.8	3
	全区	3787	3756	53.2	
七年级实验后测（八下）	同心外国语学校	167	164	66.5	1
	全区	3562	3562	52.1	

表4-8 八年级实验前后成绩与全区对比分析

八年级学科对比分析					区排名
项目	单位	总人数	参加人数	平均分（总分85分）全体	
八年级实验前测（八上）	同心外国语学校	135	99	63.01	4
	全区	3787	3756	56.4	
八年级试验后测（九下）	同心外国语学校	105	99	66.1	1
	全区	3562	3562	55.1	

根据以上两批研究对象的前测和后测均分与全区均分及排名情况，我们可以得出这样的结论：课题组开展在阅读教学课堂上培养学生的评判性思维对其阅读能力的提高是有效的。

三、访谈结果与分析

（一）研究对象访谈

在研究前后，研究人员在两批研究对象中分别抽取了9位不同英语水平的学生进行了访谈，每个层次3位学生，也就是总共18位学生。对每个研究对象使用的是非结构化的访谈，包含3个问题。以期对第一个研究问题提供补充说明和佐证。然后，研究人员将录音转化成文字，并加以整理。访谈情况如下。

（1）两届学生对英语阅读课的兴趣整体上都提高了，因为阅读课不再是枯燥地讲解课文词汇语法知识和阅读技巧，而变成了彼此的分享和讨论。

（2）在阅读课的环节中，多数学生对预测和检测环节很期待。"角色扮演让我能过一下做演员的瘾。"一个英语水平稍差的学生如是说。中等水平的学生更喜欢"分析人物情感、推测故事发展"的教学环节，因为这些让他们觉得自己很棒，可以体验当作者的感受。"故事阅读中，主人公情感分析很烧脑，但我很喜欢，之前读故事都没关注过。"

所有水平的学生对讨论环节非常喜欢。"虽然我英语不好，但是在小组讨论的时候，我也可以参与，他们会给我解释，哈哈！而且我觉得，我也可以想出很好的主意。"一个水平相对较差的学生说道。多数学生认为讨论环节可以激发他们的思考、他们的思维可以得到碰撞，能养成从多个角度理解事物、了解世界的习惯。

高水平的学生表示对角色置换、评价故事或文章、推测故事结局等活动的喜爱，他们认为，角色代入地思考问题让他们能体会故事发生的那个年代和自己生活的时代不同，而且可以养成换位思考的习惯，这样可以学会设身处地地想问题。"还有，一个好玩的地方，就是，我可以天马行空地想象，因为老师说答案不唯一。"

（3）学生对评价性的问题了解更加深入，学生认为这样的问题可以让他们深入理解故事的背景、人物、情节、主旨。"老师不仅让我们评价故事，还让我们评价作者的写作水平，嘿嘿，这个可以让我们跳出文章看问题，我的语文水平都提高了。"在教师的引导下，他们会在文中或生活中找到细节、例子去支撑他的观点，有理有据地论述自己的观点，从而使他们的思路更加开阔，更具有思辨性和逻辑性。

（二）研究人员访谈

同时，我们在研究前后，研究人员相互间也进行了访谈，采用的是非结构化访谈，包含三个问题，以期了解研究人员本身的评判性思维的水平、在阅读教学的语篇解读、目标设计、促进学生评判性思维能力发展的教学活动设计等方面的前后变化。之后，研究人员将录音转成文字，并加以整理。教师访谈结果如下。

针对访谈问题一"你的学生是否喜欢上阅读课"，所有研究人员发现，从最初的部分学生有畏难情绪到绝大部分学生喜爱上阅读课，学生上阅读课的兴趣变浓了。"从最初的畏惧阅读到慢慢尝试理解，再到深入思考阅读课上的问题，学生觉得阅读课越来越有趣，能联系生活实际，也能关注阅读展现的思想性，也越来越喜欢阅读。"一位研究人员说。还有研究人员说："大部分学生比较喜欢上阅读课，尤其是故事性强和趣味性强的文章阅读。"

　　针对问题二"你认为一节阅读课的教学目标应包括哪些方面？哪个目标最重要呢"，研究前，多数老师认为，教学目标应包括语言知识、语言技能，阅读课结束后，学生能获取文章信息、理解文章内容、复述文章等即为目标达成。但研究结束后，教师对教学目标的理解发生了变化。"英语阅读课的目标应涵盖几个方面：语言能力、文化意识、思维品质和学习能力。""在英语教学中的教学目标设计中，要深入研读文本，进行语篇分析，来设置具体的教学目标。一节课可能无法涵盖全部四个层面，但大部分会涉及三至四个层次的教学目标。我认为思维品质是其中最重要的方面。因为思维能力的发展贯穿整节课的设计。""从知识、理解、分析、评价、应用、创新不同层面进行培养。我认为思维能力的培养能促进语言能力、学习能力和文化品格的提高。"从以上教师的表述中，可以明确的是，研究人员在研究后对教学目标的理解和设定时，关注到了学生思维的发展。

　　针对问题三"你的阅读教学设计中主要培养学生的哪些能力？有关注到培养学生的评判性思维吗？（如果有）怎样设计的"，通过对研究前后教师访谈的对比发现，研究前多数教师在阅读教学设计中，关注的是学生学习语言的能力，注重词句篇章的理解，输出活动聚焦到复述，但研究后，教师在设计教学前通过用王蔷老师提出的what,how,why语篇解读方式，对阅读文章进行语篇解读后，教学设计时除了关注信息梳理，归纳结构外，还特别注意到要揣测文章和作者的意图、评价文章中的观点等培养思维尤其是评判性思维的活动。以下是部分老师的访谈内容，"我的阅读教学中，主要培养学生的阅读能力，理解、分析、推理、应用、创造等能力。获取信息只是最基础层面的能力，大部分学生经过训练之后能快速搜索关键词，从而获取关键信息。然而后续的能力培养却耗时较长。评判性思维的培养需要循序渐进，设计多样化的授课环节，如采用图表归类、图片演绎、思维导图、流程图等展示阅读文章的结构与各部分之间的关系。采用不同级别的设问引发学生的思考和讨论等，小组合作完成任务等。""在教学中，我会关注到评判性思维的培养。我是这样设计我的教学的：在读前，通过文本里的图片和标题，设置问题，引导学生进行预测，发散思维同时激活背景知识；在读中，让学生整体阅读，获取大意与细节信息，在小说、故事类文章中整理情节发展，在说明文、议论文中梳理文章结构，锻炼学生评判性思维能力的理解层次；在读后，会组织小组活动，创设情境，让学生对文本、作者观点或人物进行分析与评价，最后进行自我作品的生成与创新，这主要锻炼了学生的分析、评价与创新层次的评判思维发展。""在教学设计中，教师首先对文本进行解读，从 what、how、why 三个方面进行分析，真正读懂作者的写作意图。在教学过程中，引导学生通过对文本的理解归纳概括文本的大意。在读后，设计一些开放式的问题，比如说在 How to communicate with your parents 一课中，我设计了 'Which is the most useful way? Why？' 'What do you think of the writer's tips on communicating with your parents better?' 等问题引导学生学会赞赏或者质疑，在评价的基础上形成自己的观点和看法。在评价讨论中，学生学会以辩证的观点看待所读的内容，同时课堂也形成了一个善于分析思考、利于交流评价、乐于听取不同意见的良好氛围。"

第五章　培养学生评判性思维的研究结论

在研究归纳、总结中，我们完成以下项目：研究组进行实践后的评判性思维倾向性问卷调查；对准备阶段抽取的研究对象进行研究后的访谈；对研究人员进行了访谈，了解其阅读课教学设计及实施情况；对研究对象进行阅读能力的后测；用SPSS分析前后测成绩，用图表形式对比前后问卷，得出结论。

一、应用合适的方式发展评判性思维

在初中英语阅读教学中，教师可以通过在阅读教学活动中优化促进评判性思维发展的活动和提问方式，提高学生的阅读兴趣，促进其评判性思维的发展。评判性思维的七个维度中，评判思维倾向处于矛盾范围的学生数量明显增多，具有正性评判性思维的学生增加了，并出现了评判性思维倾向全面强的学生，而与评判性思维严重对立的学生数量明显减少。

二、在阅读教学中融入评判性思维

教师在阅读教学中设计培养学生评判性思维能力的问题和活动有助于提高学生的阅读能力。研究前后学生的整体阅读能力有了大幅提高。其中阅读能力低水平的学生数量明显减少，尤其是八年级开始参加实验的学生，经过一年半的实验，学生变化明显，这可能与九年级下学期专项训练和整体紧张有序的学习氛围有关；中等水平的学生阅读能力变化在两批研究对象中的表现最明显，这与教师优化教学设计、关注学生思维发展有关系，学生在回答有关分析、推理与揣测作者意图等阅读题目时，正确率提高；而高水平的学生数量大幅增加，但七年级开始参加实验的学生变化不明显，可能与学生在八年级的身心发生变化有关。

三、培养评判性思维的教学策略

研究成员在不断研究与实践后，总结出一些在初中英语阅读教学中培养学生评判性思维能力的教学策略。

（1）利用读前预测与假设活动，激活学生的背景、阅读图式，培养其推测能力。

（2）通过对学生的预测结果和阅读文章的结构及主旨大意的对比，帮助学生形成新的阅读图式，培养其评判能力。

（3）指导学生用思维导图的方式，梳理文章脉络更有利于学生评判性思维能力的培养。

（4）在细节阅读的研读文本推理解释活动中，教师巧妙设计问题链，培养学生的分析、解释和评价能力。

（5）读后的自评活动，帮助学生读中专注，读后反思，培养其自我监控能力。

（6）在作业设计环节，教师通过让学生模仿写作、篇章创作或故事续写等形式，培养学生的创新应用能力。

四、不同体裁的阅读文章的读后教学

研究人员还总结出了在不同体裁的阅读文章的读后环节，教师可以通过开展不同的活动，培养学生的评判性思维，具体如下。

（一）记叙文和说明文

通过设计讨论活动，让学生分小组讨论推测作者的写作意图或文章主旨大意，培养其推理能力。

通过小组合作分析评价文章的结构、描写手法及逻辑，培养学生的逻辑评判思维能力。

（二）故事小说类文章

通过对故事、小说中人物性格的评价，培养学生的评判和评价能力。

利用角色代入活动，培养学生的应用与创新能力，还能培养其多角度思考问题的能力。

通过设计后续情节预测活动，培养学生的推理与创造的能力。

通过小组讨论作者意图，培养学生的推理与情感感悟能力。

（三）议论文

通过让学生分析评价作者的论点，培养其分析与评价能力，使其形成辩证看问题的思维。

通过让学生评价论证过程的活动，培养其评估与论证的能力，并帮助其形成该主题的论证方法和框架。

在评论作者的论点和论证之后，通过设计让学生陈述个人观点的活动，培养其逻辑评判能力。

五、四种体裁评判性阅读教学流程

研究成员通过对实验过程中使用的教材——《英语（沪教牛津版）》七至九年级六本教材进行分析，发现我们教材中的语篇按体裁主要可以划分为说明文、记叙文、议论文、小说故事、诗歌等五类文章，由于诗歌仅出现了两篇，因此课题组经过语篇分析—研讨教学设计—课堂实践——研讨、反思—优化教学设计—课堂再实践—总结撰写教学设计的教研程序，针对研究中使用的教材篇章总结出记叙文、说明文、故事小说、议论文四种体裁的评判性阅读教学流程图。（图5-1至图5-4）

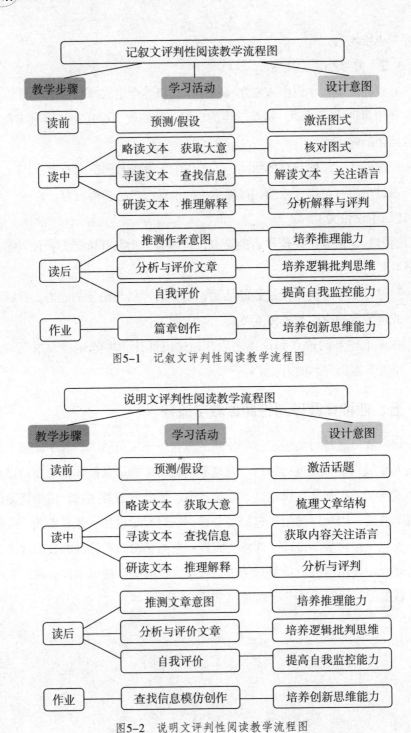

图5-1　记叙文评判性阅读教学流程图

图5-2　说明文评判性阅读教学流程图

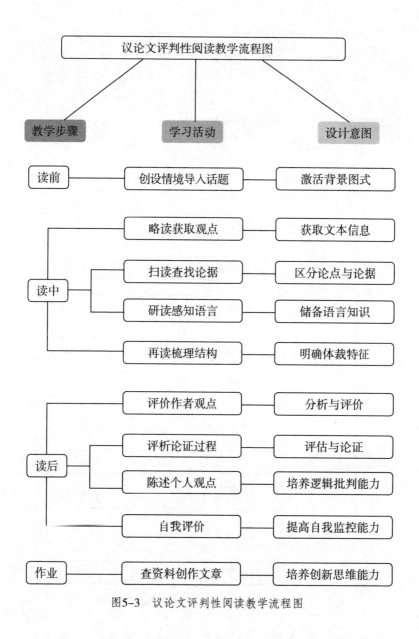

图5-3 议论文评判性阅读教学流程图

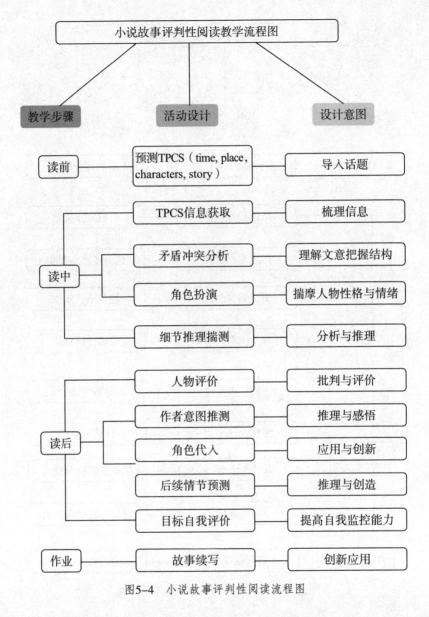

图5-4 小说故事评判性阅读流程图

不同体裁评判性思维阅读的教学流程图为课题组成员及未参加本课题研究的教师提供了备课参考，使其在设计相同体裁的阅读教学时，有意识、有次序地开展相关活动，更高效进行评判性思维培养的阅读教学。

六、评判性思维培养的问题设计

课题组成员通过研究总结出了可以促进学生评判性思维发展的一系列问题样例：

解释与分析：

Which character do you like, why?

What might you learn from ...?

How did the writer make ... so vivid?

How do you know...?

How do you solve this problem?

How do you introduce...?

How do you clarify...?

How do you prove ...?

Can you outline the similarities and differences between...and...?

分析与推理：

What can you infer from ...?

What does...really want to say?

What might be the meaning of ...?

What has led to that conclusion?

What might you learn by comparing the results of different analyses of ...?

What might be the reasoning behind ...?

What questions would you ask about... based on your own purpose?

What does...imply us?

What might be the purpose of...?

What's the purpose of the writer/ the article?

Can you write an ending for the story? What is it?

评价：

What do you think of ...?

How do you feel about...?

How do you like...?

Do you agree with the author's opinion that...?

Are you happy with the ending? Why?

Do you think the solution is good? Why?

创造：

If you were..., what would you do?

How might you continue the story?

What would you do if you were there?

What would life be like without ....?

How might you construct an argument to support your point?

How can you improve...?

本研究总结出了一些培养评判性思维能力发展的教学策略、不同体裁文章中培养学生的评判性思维的读后活动设计，如在记叙文和说明文中通过讨论或者小组合作活动培养学生评判、推理能力等；归纳出了基于深圳初中英语教材（沪教牛津版）四种体裁文章的评判性阅读教学流程。这些策略和流程给对评判性阅读感兴趣却无从下手的教师提供了具体的参考和指导。作者总结罗列出的有利于培养评判性思维的一系列问题样例，给老师们提供了范本和指南，让学生在学习过程中从被动接受变为主动思考，从根本上改变其学习态度，不再只是死板关注语言知识和语言技能，而忽略阅读材料传递的情感态度和价值取向，以及对问题的深入思考。同时，让学生感受到阅读的乐趣，带着问题去阅读文章，学会分析、推理、评价，不是被动填鸭式接受学习内容，经过自身思考、加工，内化为自己的思想和能力，不盲从阅读材料观点，按照标准进行清晰、灵活、相关的思考与分析，并达到一定的逻辑性和深刻性，强化好奇、开放、自信、正直和坚毅等人格特质，对学生形成良好的思维习惯，生活中能多进行推理分析，明辨是非，形成自己正确的人生观和价值观有很大的帮助。授人以鱼不如授人以渔，学生学会正确的学习方法和科学的思维方法才能养成终身学习的好习惯。与此同时，主动思考强化了学习过程，促进了学习效率的提高，从而使其阅读能力得到了提升，学习效果有了显著的改变。

初中英语阅读教学目前仍然进行一定程度上的应试教育，这是中考的必然结果。英语学科核心素养要求对学生进行全方位、长远的教育。该研究以核心素养为指导，努力以阅读课的教学为例，提升学生各方面的素养，同时促进评判性思维这一创新型国家的要求得以培养。理论指导下的教学过程需要不断摸索，课题组成员通过不断地阅读并消化理论，讨论设计可行的教学策略和教学流程，并在实际课程中不断完善，优化了教学效果，让课堂更有深度，学生从单纯的阅读到思考有深度的问题，学会质疑，学会探究，学会总结，熟练运用理解、分析、应用、评估等技能，并内化价值观，操练知识点和技能。教师备课更加认真深入，自己先深入理解文本，并从结构、理念、情感态度等多方面进行思考，精心设问，由易到难，引导学生一步步从表面的信息点获取到深入的文本特征、规律探索、观念评估、价值指向等多方面深层次理解，最终举一反三，形成自己的认知体系，并通过解释、推理、评价、自我监控进行深入学习，提升思维。

培养评判性思维的阅读课堂需要教师首先具有相关的理论知识，为此，课题组的老师们认真研读相关理论书籍，用先进的理论武装自己，学习评判性思维设问方式，不断进行理论学习、教法探究、效果分析、策略调整等研究性活动，寻找不同类型的阅读材料，对学生进行不同领域阅读材料的训练，大大提升了教师的教学能力和专业素养，由满堂灌的陈旧教学模式，转为以学生为主体，以阅读材料和生活为载体，不断联系生活实际，引导学生探究阅读内容的内涵，而非止步于语言知识和语言技能的学习，让学习变得更有实际意义，课堂充满乐趣，学生乐于思考，评判性思维得到训练，教师包容性、开放性更强，接纳不同的思维方式和不同程度的进步，设计问题更加有梯度，尊重每个学生不同的基础学识和对问题的认识。为学生提供更广阔的平台，激发学生深入思考，学会评判的能力。课堂也因此变得更有趣、更高效。

在此过程中，教师专业素养得到发展，教学能力得到提升，教学效果得到提高，课题组成员参与各种赛课和论文比赛，获得了各种奖项，促进了教师的长远发展。与此同时，学生感受更深入的课堂，学习内容变得更有方法性。经过调查问卷和访谈，发现学生的评判性思维倾向显著提升，阅读成绩也因此快速进步。研究所总结的教学策略和流程具有可操作性，取得了实实在在的效果，极大促进教师和学生的发展。

本研究团队在阅读国内外文献的基础上商讨教学策略，实践出一些教学设计和不同体裁的教学流程图，课题组成员参与了各级各类公开课、赛课、论文评比，以期侧重学生英语阅读中评判性思维的培养，实践英语学科核心素养中的思维品质培养，从长远培养学生的思维能力，以应对日新月异的未来。对心智不成熟、知识结构尚在搭建阶段的初中生而言，这项研究的开展艰难重重，课题组成员一一克服，但仍有一些方面需要完善。

（1）从教师访谈结果中反映出教师自身的评判性思维能力还需要提高，基于阅读文本设计评判性思维问题和活动的能力仍需加强，这需要更多相关领域的专业性培训和案例学习。

（2）学生处于青春期，心理稳定性较弱，个性较强，学习过程中的效果有少许随机性质。实验结果也呈现波动状态，而非直线上升，与该阶段学生的心理特点密切相关。

（3）如果能设计出学生活动手册，完善学案，并附以学生作品集将更能展现评判性思维的实现步骤和效果。

（4）该研究囊括了初中阶段英语课本上的文章，如果能因人施教，选择研究对象更感兴趣的阅读文章，并对学生个体进行跟踪研究，展现该研究对学生长期思维的影响，则更有意义。

参考文献

[1] Bhatia V K. Genre analysis, ESP and professional practice [J]. English for Specific Purposes, 2008, 27（2）: 0–174.

[2] Facione P A. The DelPhi Report Critical Thinking: A Statement of Expert Consensus for Purposes of Educational Assessment and

Instruction［R］. Millbrae CA: The California Academic Press, 1990.

［3］Fahim M, Bagherkazemi M, Alemi M. The Relationship between Test Takers, Critical Thinking Ability and their Performance on the Reading Section of TOEFL［J］. Journal of Language Teaching & Research, 2010, 1（6）: 830–837.

［4］Halpern D F. Assessing the Effectiveness of Critical Thinking Instruction［J］. The Journal of General Education, 2001.（4）:270–286.

［5］Hassani M T, Rahmany R, Babaei M. The Relationship between Iranian EFL Learners' Critical Thinking and Reading Comprehension Performance in Journalistic Texts［J］. Theory & Practice in Language Studies, 2013, 3（10）:1873–1878.

［6］Paul R, Elder L. The Miniature Guide to Critical Thinking: Concepts and Tools［M］. Dillon Beach, CA: The Foundation for Critical Thinking, 2008.

［7］程晓堂，赵思奇. 英语学科核心素养的实质内涵［J］. 课程·教材·教法，2016（5）：79–86.

［8］戴聪萍. 基于思维品质培养的高中英语阅读教学设问策略［J］. 英语教师，2017（6）：132–133.

［9］胡明勇. 大学生英语自主学习中的自我评价［J］. 外语，2010（11）：111，113.

［10］景晶. 关于高中英语阅读教学评判性思维能力培养的思考［J］. 课程教育研究：外语学法教法研究，2018（26）：135.

［11］李迎新，谢丽敏，袁园等. 基于评判性思维层级理论的大学英语教学［J］. 石家庄学院学报，2017（1）：151–156.

［12］秦秀白. 体裁教学法述评［J］. 外语教学与研究，2000（1）：42–46.

［13］沈爱芬. 思维导图在初中英语阅读教学中的运用［J］. 中小学外

语教学（中学篇），2014（5）：12-16.

[14] 王后雄."问题链"的类型及教学功能 ——以化学教学为例
[J].教育科学研究，2010（5）：52-56.

[15] 王蔷.从综合语言运用能力到英语学科核心素养——高中英语课
程改革的新挑战 [J].英语教师，2015（16）：6-7.

[16] 王式街.英语课堂中基于提问的思维品质培养 [J].基础外语教
育，2015，17（4）：89-93.

[17] 王学鹏.英语阅读思维品质的培养策略 [J].教学与管理，2017
（10）：48-50.

[18] 文秋芳.论外语专业研究生高层次思维能力的培养 [J].学位与
研究生教育，2008（10）：29-34.

[19] 文秋芳，王建卿，赵彩然，等.构建我国外语类大学生思辨能力
量具的理论框架 [J].外语界，2009（1）：37-43.

[20] 易荣榴，陈书元.利用英语阅读文本，培养中学生批判性思维能
力 [J].中小学英语教学与研究，2017（2）：46.

[21] 章策文.高中英语阅读教学与学生思维能力的培养 [J].现代基
础教育研究，2017（1）：106-109.

[22] 张春柏，舒运祥.义务教育教科书英语七年级上、下册 [M].
上海：上海教育出版社，2013.

[23] 张春柏，舒运祥.义务教育教科书英语八年级上、下册 [M].
上海：上海教育出版社，2014.

[24] 张春柏，舒运祥.义务教育教科书英语九年级上、下册 [M].
上海：上海教育出版社，2017.

[25] 张若兰.英语精读教学中的思维训练 [J].韩山师范学院学报，
1996（4）：76-79.

第六章　例析评判性思维能力培养的策略

一、引言

《义务教育英语课程标准（2022年版）》明确指出，思维品质指认的思维个性特征，反映学生在理解、分析、比较、推断、批判、评价、创造等方面的层次和水平。思维品质的提升有助于学生学会发现问题、分析问题和解决问题，以及对事物作出正确的价值判断（教育部，2022）。

评判性思维能力（critical thinking skills）是思维能力中的重要组成部分，是指"运用恰当的评价标准，进行有意识的思考，最终做出有理据的判断"（转引自文秋芳，2012）。评判性思维是指在解决问题过程中表现出来的解读、分析、推理、评价、解释和自我监控能力的高低（包丰，2019）。初中英语阅读教学是学生学习语言知识、获取信息、感知文化的重要途径，也是培养评判性思维能力的重要途径。

二、初中英语阅读教学存在的问题

自课标（2017年版）明确英语学科素养包含思维品质以来，越来越多的一线教师开始关注学生思维品质的培养，但在教学实践中仍然存在以下问题。

（1）重点放在词句上，缺乏根据上下文语境分析推断词意的活动。

（2）教学活动多在获取信息层面，忽略对作者写作意图与观点的分析。

（3）学生阅读文本的时间不充分，缺乏对文本本身的深层解读及对文本的架构与逻辑合理性评判的活动。

（4）有讨论环节，但教师设定固定答案，限制了学生的想象力与思维活跃性。

（5）作业设计与所学内容无关，无法培养其迁移创新的能力，思维无法延展。

三、基于评判性思维能力培养的教学活动实践

陈则航（2019）指出，批判性思维的培养要融入阅读的各个阶段，教师需要不断启发学生去思考。本文将以《英语（沪教牛津版）》七年级下册Module 4 Colourful life Unit 8中一篇阅读课My lifetime hobby—studying stars的教学设计为例，探讨基于评判性思维能力培养的教学活动设计策略。

（一）教学内容分析

本文是Patrick Moore写的一篇小短文，文中介绍了他小时候的爱好——夜晚和妈妈一起看星星，长大后成了一名著名的电视节目主持人的成长经历，他鼓励大家把自己喜欢的事情做到极致，变成自己的事业。

（二）学情分析

学生经过了近一个学期的评判性思维训练，其评判性思维处于发展阶段，有一定的思维能力；语言知识方面，有了一定的词汇积累，能独立阅读并概括主要内容；对主题内容并不陌生，已经学过介绍个人及他人的话题，对表述兴趣爱好的话题比较熟悉；有独立思考的习惯和小组合作的意识。但其对比分析评价作者的写作结构和意图的能力尚不足。

（三）目标设定

基于对文本内容和学生情况分析，本节课设定的教学目标如下。

经过本节课的学习，学生能够：①通过阅读，获取Patrick Moore爱好的有关信息，如小时候爱做的事，长大后自己成功的事业，给读者的建议等；②梳理Patrick的故事脉络，建构结构化知识；③运用所获得的内容信息，对比分析故事叙述结构；④分析、评价Patrick的建议与观点，推断兴趣变成事业的关键要素。

（四）教学过程

本节课按常规分为三个教学环节：读前环节、读中环节、读后环节。教学设计框架如图6-1所示。

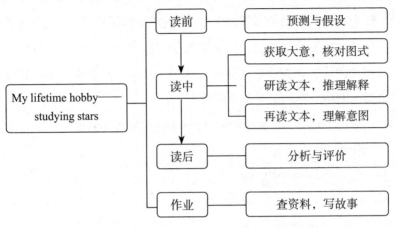

图6-1　教学设计思维导图

笔者在读前、读中、读后三个环节中分别设计了不同活动，让学生积极参与其中，逐步逐层培养学生的阅读能力和批判思维能力。

活动一：预测与假设

读前环节的主要目的是激发学生阅读兴趣、设置悬念，为读中环节做铺垫。预测要求学生结合已有的背景知识，对文本可能讨论的话题进行猜测，是一种积极的思维过程（赵旭辉，2017）。兴趣爱好是学生熟悉的话题，因此在读前环节，笔者首先向学生展示了一张自己旅游的图片，并告诉他们笔者的爱好就是旅游，然后问，"What's your hobby？"再展示Patrick Moore与本文的题目"My lifetime hobby—studying stars"及课文图片，让学生采用头脑风暴法预测文章内容，教学片段如下。

T: What information can you get from the title and the pictures?

S1: The text talks about hobby.

S2: It talks about studying stars.

T: Please pay attention to the word "lifetime". What does that mean?

S3: "一辈子"！No, it's in his life.

S4: His whole life.

S5: He likes his hobby in his whole life.

然后是 "What would you write if you were the writer?（假如你是文章的作者，你会在你的文章中写些什么？）"这样的问题设计，比直接看题目预测内容让学生更有代入感，既能激发学生思考的主动性，也可以培养学生谋篇布局的能力，为读后环节做好铺垫。在这个环节中，学生边回答，教师边把关键信息罗列记录在黑板的左侧。

T: Great! What would you write if you were the writer?

S1: What is the hobby?

S2: When did the hobby start?

S3: Why did he have the hobby?

S4: How did he study stars?

设计意图：预测活动旨在培养学生的推理能力。本文话题与学生生活贴近，对于处在这个充满好奇心年龄的学生来说，由教师本人及同学的爱好引入，可以快速激发他们的兴趣，为顺利阅读做好准备。背景知识对学生的习得体验非常重要，利用插图和问题导入，让学生预测文章内容，能激发学生的阅读兴趣，激活已有图式，搭建旧知识与新知识之间的桥梁，推断文章内容的可能性，活跃其思维。"假设你是本文作者"这个环节，比直接看题目预测内容更能够激发学生思维主动性，激活学生原有的写作图式，培养学生谋篇布局的能力，为读后分析评价文章结构做好基础铺垫。

活动二：获取大意，核对图式

读中环节是阅读课的核心。教师可以在本环节培养学生的多种思维能力。快速浏览，获取文章大意是阅读技能中的微技能之一，这种阅读策略可以帮助学生理清文章结构，培养其整体阅读能力。在此环节，笔者考虑到学生的概括能力还处于起始阶段，因而让学生先自己总结陈述，再给出匹配任务。学生在完成任务的过程中，自我监控修正自己的表述，形成新的图式。

学生的概括示例如下。

Para.1 The beginning of his hobby.

Para.2 He used to watch the sky with his mom on clear nights.

Para.3 The TV program has lasted more than 50 years.

Para.4 Anybody can turn their hobbies into careers.

之后，教师在PPT上给出匹配选项的任务，让学生进行段落与大意之间的匹配。任务如图6-2所示。

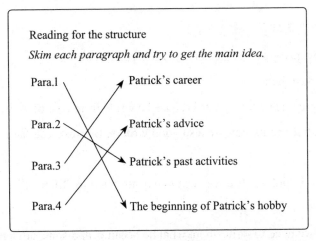

图6-2　段落与大意匹配

学生明确了各部分大意之后，就弄清了文章的结构内容，然后再和读前活动中的"假设自己是作者"所列的写作内容（笔者在把活动一中学生所列内容写在黑板左侧）进行对比分析，分析自己的写作图式与作者的写作框架之间孰优孰劣，形成同类话题的较佳写作图式。对比图式如图6-3所示。

Compare your outline with the main ideas:

Be a good writer	Main idea of each paragraph
What is the hobby?	Para.1 The beginning of Patrick's hobby
When did the hobby start?	Para.2 Patrick's past activities on clear nights
Why did he have the hobby?	Para.3 Patrick's career
How did he study stars?	Para.4 Patrick's advice

图6-3　学生写作框架与文章大意对比

教学片段示例：

T：Hey guys, who is the better writer, you or Patrick?

S1: Maybe, he is.

S2: I agree. He wrote better because he wrote from past till now.

T: Yes, but I think you are also good writers. Because you list most of what he wrote.

S3: Yes, I think so. But we need to pay attention to "lifetime".

T: So?

S4: So we need to write about what he became, and some advice.

T: Do you think we need add something more to make it better?

S5: Maybe we can write about what he studied in his university!

T: Wow! Great idea! I absolutely agree! We should write about what he studied in his university.

设计意图：本环节通过让学生快速阅览整篇文章，获取每段主旨大意，培养其解读文本的能力，也是培养其批判性思维能力之解读能力。笔者让学生先自己概括、解释，然后让其通过对比自己的概括与给出匹配项之间的不同，自我修正答案，这个过程既培养了他们的自我监控能力又帮助其梳理清文章脉络。在与读前预设对比评价环节，笔者运用追问的方式，引导学生调控答案，并给出自己的建议，为同类话题的写作的谋篇布局形成新的图式！

活动三：研读文本，推理解释

在学生获得文章大意、梳理清文章脉络之后，教师应引导学生潜心研读文章，进一步理解文章内容细节要点、分清文中的事实与观点、解释对文本解读和分析的过程、评价作者的观点。教师可以在这一系列的文本解读的过程，设计有层次的问题链，培养学生批判性思维技能中的分析、推理、评价和解释能力。笔者在文本解读的基础上，设置了递进式问题链，推动学生由浅层到深度的思维发展。

（1）What made Patrick begin to like studying stars?

（2）What did he use to do on clear nights?

（3）What did he think of the stars?

（4）How did he turn his hobby into his career?

（5）Why can his program last so long?

（6）What does the word lively mean? How do you know that?

（7）What advice does he give? Do you agree?

设计意图：问题链的设计有利于学生思维的深度性和延续性的发展。在本环节中，笔者设计了信息获取与理解（浅层）和分析解释与判断（深层）两个层次的问题链：问题1~3属于低阶思维问题链，主要围绕Patrick的兴趣爱好、小时候做些什么、他对星空的描述等信息获取设置，这些信息的提取为接下来的文本深度解析、推断和评价搭建了支架；问题4~7属于高阶思维问题链，通过让学生分析Patrick怎样把爱好变成事业、解释他的节目可以长盛不衰的理由、通过语境猜词义、评价Patrick的建议这些问题，两个层次的问题环环相扣、由浅至深，逐步提升难度，学生的分析、推理、解释和评价能力在此过程中得到运用与发展。

活动四：再读文本，解读意图

周智忠（2017）指出，如何引导学生识别作者观点并合理质疑，对培养学生的批判性思维能力十分重要。而解读是进行批判质疑和反思的前提和基础。解读需要借助于分析和推理，充分的解读也有利于进一步地分析和推理（董焱，2017）。解读作者意图可以帮助学生与文本对话，能更好地理解文本所传达的信息。在此活动中，笔者引导学生再研读最后一段，采用小组合作方式就作者的写作意图进行讨论、解读，笔者与小组成员问答示例。

T: Why did Patrick write this story?

Group 1: He wanted to show us his hobby. And wanted to tell us to have a hobby and enjoy what we do.

T: Brilliant! Why did Patrick write lifetime hobby and asked us enjoy what we do?

Group 2: Hobby is very important, but "坚持" is more important.

T: You mean stick with our hobby!

Group 3: The writer encourages us to find our hobby and turn them into our future career.

T: Exactly!

设计意图：在学生充分研读文本获取知识、文本架构、细节信息等基础上，教师引导学生推断作者意图与隐含意义可以培养其解读、推断能力。本活动中，笔者采用小组合作讨论的方式，一方面可以让学生相互激发活跃思维，另一方面可以培养学生的自我调控能力。

活动五：分析与评价

读后活动是让学生充分内化文本知识与内涵之后，教师为帮助学生架构自己与文本，自己与世界的沟通桥梁而设计的活动。教师应从评价文本结构、是否认同文中观点等角度设计问题。而针对故事题材的文章，教师设计对故事中人物的评价是一种常见的读后活动。本活动中笔者设计了两组问题，学生先小组讨论，再由代表汇报。问题如下。

1. What do you think of Patrick? Do you want to be such a person?

2. What do you think of the story? Do you believe you can turn your dream into you future career?

针对第二组问题，学生讨论后只有一组同学提出了质疑，学生的回答汇总如下。

From the story, we know Patrick liked watching stars in the sky when he was young. And he said "When he learnt a little, he wanted to find out more and more". But does it "有联系" *his career—A TV programme host? Yes, he is very hard-working, persevering, but we think he is also lucky.* "运气" *is very important.* "天时、地利、人和才成就了他。"

对此回答，笔者表示非常棒，但没有立即明确表示反对与赞同。尽管由于词汇的限制，学生的回答中有汉语出现，但学生的思维方式显然是批判性思维。

设计意图：评价是独立思考、批判性思维走向自成品的关键，是我们从求知到质疑，再到分析，最终产生自己的评价的重要的一步（董焱，2017）。第一组问题让学生小组讨论评价对主人公Patrick的看法，并询问学生是否想成为这样的人，这需要学生在内化文本内容之后，提出有理有据的评价，正是批判性思维技能中评价能力的集中体现；第二组问题是引导和培养学生要有质疑权威的勇气和意识，为使这个环节能顺利进行，笔者在组织阅读前没有讲任何关于作者的背景知识，以便减轻学生的心理负担。笔者引导学生从自身和身边朋友及已知的真实故事角度考量Patrick故事的说服力和真实性，一方面可以促使学生从内化的文本中找依据，另一方面可以引导通过已有认识和经验找证据，培养其逻辑思辨能力。

活动六：作业布置

笔者认为，作业的功能有两个：一是对本节课所学内容的巩固与检测；二是对本节课知识与能力的拓展。优秀的作业设计不仅能对所学知识起到巩固检测作用，还能把课堂中的思维延续到课外，发挥学生主体思维的作用。笔者设计的家庭作业如下。

1. Please search the Internet to find out more information about Patrick and tell whether his story is credible or not.

2. Write a short story about your hobby and your future career.

设计意图：要求学生上网查找本文作者的更多信息并再次评价故事

的可信度是鼓励学生跳出文本，通过搜索更多的相关信息，学会多角度看问题，做到有理有据地评判。这一作业的设计也是针对最后一个问题的回应，引导通过更多信息与证据的查找，再全面地评价Patrick这个人和这篇文章，做到批判性思维的延续性和深刻性。而写出自己的爱好和将来有可能的事业这一任务，一方面可以帮助学生巩固运用本节课所学语言知识、文本结构；另一方面可以让其深度思考，学会规划自己的未来并从现在打好基础，也可以达成教材编者选择此文章的用意。

四、结语

在初中阅读教学中，教师通过运用某些策略优化活动设计，培养学生的解读、分析、推理、评价、解释和自我监控能力等评判性思维技能是可行的，但教师要注意以下几个方面：教师本身应具有评判性思维能力倾向，明确评判性思维技能的具体内容；评判性思维能力的培养活动应在学生充分内化文本之后才能进展顺利，因此，评判性思维活动通常重点放在一堂课的后半部分，甚至延续到第二节课；教师应为学生创设轻松愉快的课堂氛围，学生的思维才能活跃与拓展，评判性思维活动才能顺利开展；评判性思维能力的培养是循序渐进的，需要教师坚持不懈地刺激与引导。

参考文献

［1］包丰.初中英语阅读教学中培养学生批判性思维的实践［J］.中小学外语教学（中学篇），2019（1）：8-13.

［2］陈则航.批判性阅读与批判性思维培养［J］.中国外语教育（季刊），2015（2）：4-11.

［3］陈则航，王蔷，钱小芳.论英语学科核心素养中的思维品质及其发展途径［J］.课程·教材·教法，2019（1）：91-98.

［4］董焱.基于批判性思维子技能的高中英语阅读教学设计思考［G］.江苏省教育学会年会文集，2017：47-53.

［5］中华人民共和国教育部.义务教育英语课程标准（2011年版）

［M］.北京：北京师范大学出版社，2012.

［6］中华人民共和国教育部.义务教育英语课程标准（2022年版）
［M］.北京：北京师范大学出版社，2022：5.

［7］文秋芳.中国外语类大学生思辨能力现状研究［M］.北京：外语
教学与研究出版社，2012.

［8］张成年，金毅，王燕，等.英语阅读教学中的评判性思维：阐释
与评鉴［M］.杭州：浙江大学出版社，2012.

［9］赵旭辉.初中英语听说课教学中培养学生思维能力的策略［J］.
中小学外语教学（中学篇），2017（12）：51–55.

［10］周智忠.指向学生思维品质发展的初中英语阅读教学［J］.中小
学外语教学（中学篇），2017（9）：28–38.

［11］袁晶.在以读促写中培养学生的思维品质［J］.中小学外语教学
（中学篇），2019（1）：13–17.

下 篇

评判性阅读教学
设计案例

第七章 记叙文评判性阅读教学案例

案例1：A blind man and his "eyes" in a fire教学设计

——沪教牛津版七年级下Unit 3 Reading

【语篇研读】

What：

A blind man and his "eyes" in a fire是一篇小故事，详细记述了一位盲人及其导盲犬在宾馆的突发火灾中互助逃生的故事。文章首先交代了故事发生的时间、地点及主要人物：一天、宾馆、约翰（盲人）和查理（导盲犬）。接着文章记述了故事发生的开端：约翰和查理在宾馆登记入住，接待员误以为查理是约翰的宠物，因此不允许查理入内，约翰解释自己是盲人，而查理是自己的导盲犬，由此接待员道歉后将查理和约翰带到房间。接下来文章详述了故事的发展：疲惫的约翰入睡后，宾馆突发火灾，查理大声吠叫唤醒约翰，并帮助约翰在火灾中开展自救。最后是故事的结局部分：救护车到来后，消防员将约翰救出宾馆，却不想救出查理，约翰不同意丢下查理，最后约翰和查理均获救。本故事凸显了"动物是人类的好朋友"这一主题。

Why：

作者通过讲述盲人及其导盲犬在火灾中互助逃生的故事，引出"动物是人类的好朋友"这一主题，引发读者思考人类应该如何与动物相处。

How：

该文是一篇记叙文，运用一般过去时详述了盲人与其导盲犬互助求生的故事。第一部分（第1~3段）介绍了故事发生的时间、地点、主要人物及故事的开端，其中包含许多直接引语，增强了故事的真实性；第二部分（第4段）详细记述了故事发生的过程，用一系列的动词进行了细节描写，如fell asleep, started barking, woke up, smelt smoke, come in, put等，该部分是导盲犬查理对主人约翰的帮助；第三部分（第5段）是故事的结局，消防车到来后，消防员只想救出约翰，不愿将查理救出，在约翰的坚持下，最终约翰和查理均获救。

【学习目标】

1. 获取梳理本故事的事实性信息（如故事发生的时间、地点、人物及开端、发展、结局等）。

2. 梳理归纳文章结构，了解故事的要素，形成阅读及写作图式。

3. 根据故事情节分析讨论所给问题，全面辩证地评价事件及主要角色，提高评判性思维能力。

4. 通过小组合作，将故事改编成剧本，并分角色表演。

5. 分析推理作者意图，形成与动物和谐相处的态度。

【学情分析】

授课对象是七年级下学期的学生，学生在英语学习中有较高的课堂参与度，且经过半年多的学习，学生已经掌握了一定的词汇量。本课是个小故事，难度不是很大，且学生对故事性文本较感兴趣，因此在信息获取方面问题不大。但是学生在一节课40分钟内进行评价、推理思考及语言表达等，还是具有一定的挑战性的。

【教学过程】

Step 1: Pre-reading

1. Lead in

Students solve a riddle.

"It has four legs and a tail.

It can bark.

It can help the blind people."

Purpose: To arouse students' interest in this lesson and lead in today's topic: guide dogs.

2. Brainstorming

Students brainstorm how guide dogs help the blind in real life.

Purpose: To encourage students to think widely and get them ready for reading the story.

3. Predicting

Students skim the title, the introduction part and the pictures to make predictions and answer the following questions.

（1）What's the meaning of "eyes" in the title?

（2）What is the genre of the article?

（3）What may happen in the story?

Purpose: To activate students' prior schema about stories of this topic.

Step 2: While-reading

1. Reading for the main idea

Students skim the story and find out what the story is about.

Purpose: To get the main idea of the story.

2. Reading for plot

Students read the story and fill in the table to find out the necessary elements of stories.

Or they can draw their own mind map or plot.

表7-1　A blind man and his "eyes" in a fire

Time		
Place		
Main characters		
The main plots of the story	Beginning	
	Development	
	Ending	

After finishing their task, they share in groups and then in class.

Purpose: To check whether students can find out the necessary elements of the story, including the time, place, main characters, the beginning, the development and the ending and know the structure of the text.

3. Comparing and evaluating

Students compare their ideas with the plot to analyse who is the better writer.

Purpose: To check whether their prediction is correct and form the new schema.

4. Adapting and role-playing

Students read and adapt the last two paragraphs into a short play in groups and act it out.

One or two groups show in class.

Purpose: To activate students' interest in learning English and get as many students as possible involved in the learning process.

Step 3: Post-reading

Evaluating and inferring:

Students think about the following questions and share their opinions. They can give reasons from the text.

（1）What do you think of John and Charlie?

（2）Why did the author write the story?

（3）What can you learn from the story?

Purpose: To improve students' skills of critical thinking through making evaluation and inference while reading.

Step 4: Self–assessment

Please tick the sentence if you agree.

※I can get the main elements: when, where, who,what and how.

※I can understand the main plot of the story: they stayed in a hotel—a fire happened—they saved each other.

※I can retell the story according to the plot.

※I can find evidence to support my idea.

※I can form the idea that animals are friends to human beings and we should live in harmony with them.

Purpose: To check whether the objectives are achieved or not and strengthen students' self-monitoring ability.

Step 5: Homework

Choose one task from the following two writing tasks.

1. Watch a film called *A dog's purpose* and write about what you think about the relationship between human beings and animals.

2. Write your story with your own pet dog or other pets.

Purpose: To get students to think further about the relationship between human beings and animals and to cultivate students' ability of creative thinking.

案例2：My lifetime hobby—studying stars教学设计

——沪教牛津版七年级下Unit 8 Reading

【语篇研读】

What：

本文是一篇由Patrick Moore写的自传记叙文，文中介绍了Patrick Moore一生的爱好和事业。Patrick Moore介绍他在八岁时得到了一本有关星星的书，从此研究星星成了他一生的爱好。他常常和妈妈在晴朗的夜晚观测星星和天空。他形容天空就像是布满钻石的天鹅绒，有时他还能看到流星雨。作者写道，研究星星成就了他现在的事业——电视节目《星空》主持人。他热爱自己的工作，因为他能把自己所学的知识用一种生动的方式告诉听众。Patrick所主持的电视节目已经持续了50年，他因此而感到骄傲。在文章的最后，Patrick 鼓励大家要热爱自己所做之事，并要大家相信，我们每个人都可以把爱好变成事业，都可以实现自己的梦想。

Why：

作者通过介绍自己如何把小时候的梦想变成一生事业的故事，鼓励读者要有自己的爱好，要相信任何人都可以把爱好变成职业、实现自己的梦想。

How：

该文是一篇记叙文。文章共四段：第一段，作者介绍了自己爱好起因；第二段描述了小时候观测星空的习惯和景象；第三段介绍了他如何把爱好变成了一生的事业；最后，作者鼓励大家要有爱好和梦想。

作者运用一般过去时和一般现在时两种时态，按照时间顺序描述了他的爱好、事业和期望。在叙述小时候的经历时，用到了when引导的时间状语从句；用"used to do sth."描写了和妈妈过去经常做的事情；用"look like..."形容天空的样子；用"turn...into..."，"achieve one's dream"期望大家能相信自己可以把爱好变为事业从而成就梦想。

【学习目标】

1. 通过阅读，获取Patrick Moore一生爱好的有关信息，如小时候爱做的事，长大后自己成功的事业，给读者的建议等。

2. 梳理Patrick的故事脉络，建构结构化知识。

3. 运用所获得的内容信息，对比分析故事叙述结构。

4. 分析、评价Patrick的建议与观点，推理兴趣变成事业的关键要素。

【学情分析】

根据皮亚杰认知发展理论，七年级下学期的学生处于形式运算阶段（12~15岁）的初期，抽象思维开始占优势，经过近一年的批判性阅读训练，其思维的独立性、概括性和批判性处于发展阶段，有了一定的概括能力和批判性思维能力。英语知识方面，他们已经积累了一定的词汇量，能独自阅读与其词汇量匹配的文章，并能概括其主要内容。学习本课前，学生已经学习过介绍个人及他人的话题，话题中包括了兴趣爱好，因而他们具有本课话题的文化背景及语言知识，这对顺利达成学习目标有很大的帮助；学生有较好的独立思考的习惯，有小组活动的经验，课堂表现积极活跃。

【教学过程】

Step 1: Pre-reading

1. Predicting

Students read the title, and the pictures. And then predict what the writer talks about.

2. Assumption

Teacher asks students to think and brainstorm the question

If you were Patrick, what would you write?

Teacher will write answers on the blackboard.

Purpose: To activate students' back-ground knowledge and their previous reading and writing schema about hobby.

Step 2: While–reading

1. Reading for the main idea

Skim the story and tell what it mainly tells us.

Patrick turned his lifetime hobby—studying stars into_____, and he encouraged us to _____ and try our best to _____.

Purpose: To develop students' reading skill—skimming and get the main idea of the story.

2. Reading for the structure

Students skim each paragraph and try to get the main idea. Teacher shows them the ideas and asks them to match them with each paragraph.

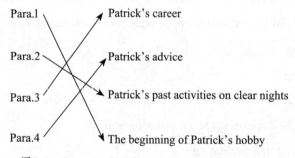

图7-1　Corresponding diagram of paragraph and structure

Purpose: To develop students' critical thinking. Students can form a new reading & writing schema by comparing their previous schema（written on the blackboard）with the story's structure.

3. Comparing and evaluating

Students compare their ideas with the main ideas to analyse who is the better writer.

Purpose: Teacher uses question chain to develop students' thinking. The first three questions are designed to get basic information, which belong to low order thinking. Questions 4~6 belong to high order thinking.

4. Reading for details

Students read the story again and answer questions:

（1）Why did Patrick like to study stars?

（2）Did he watch the sky on clear nights?

（3）How did he think about the stars?

（4）Did he turn his hobby into his career easily?

（5）What's his advice? Do you agree?

Purpose: Let the students have a deep understanding of the story.

Step 3: Post-reading

1. Retelling

Students work in groups of 4 to retell the story according to the given information.

Purpose: To help students apply what they have learnt and develop their logical thinking.

2. Inferring

Students work in groups to infer why Patrick wrote this story?

Purpose: To develop students' inferring ability.

3. Analyzing and evaluating

Ss work in groups and discuss the following questions:

（1）What do you think of Patrick? Do you want to be such a person?

（2）"Anybody can achieve their dream." Do you agree? Why or why not?

（3）To achieve our dreams, what else can we do?

Purpose: To develop students' analyzing and evaluating abilities.

Step 4: Self-assessment

Please tick the sentence if you agree.

※I can get the specific information about Patrick's lifetime hobby.

※I can get the main idea of the story.

※I can make an outline when I write a story about my hobby.

※I can retell Patrick's story according to the key words.

※I can understand the importance of having a hobby.

※I know how I can turn my hobby into my future career.

Purpose: To check whether the goals are achieved or not.

Step 5: Homework

1. Read the story aloud.

2. Write your story. The following questions may help you:

（1）What is your hobby?

（2）What is your dream?

（3）How will you achieve your dream?

Purpose: To practise what students have learnt and cultivate students' problem-solving ability.

案例3：The king and the rice教学设计

——沪教牛津版八年级上Unit 2 Reading

【语篇研读】

What：

The king and the rice是一个关于数字的故事，国王与智者下棋，并承诺若智者赢得比赛可以要任何奖品。智者提出要米粒作为赢棋奖品，且米粒需按其要求摆放，即每个格子的米粒数量都是上一个格子的两倍。最后，智者赢得了比赛，国王让侍者拿上米，却发现即使用整个国家的米也远不够所需米粒。

Why:

通过描述国王与智者下棋的故事，让读者了解到古代智者对数字的认识，同时也通过计算每个得数的由来$2^{(n-1)}$，让读者感受到数字的奥秘；通过人物的语言和动作描述，推测和总结人物性格特点；以及学会谨慎做出承诺。

How:

本文是一篇记叙文。一共6段，分为三个部分。第一部分（第1~2段），作者介绍了国王挑战智者进行了一场对弈。第二部分（第3~5段），国王承诺给智者他想要的米。第三部分（第6段），国王输了比赛，他意识到没有足够的米给智者。

作者在文章中分别使用了两张图片，图一是智者与国王在宫殿里下棋；图二展示了一个棋盘，上面标了点和数字，依次是1，2，4，8，16，32，64，128，256，512，…

全文使用一般过去时，作者用表示故事时间线的词和短语one day，for a long time，finally展现故事的发展；用动词词组challenge... to...，promise...，order... to...，realize...描写故事的主要情节；用You can ... if...和If..., I'd like....两个if引导的从句描写这场博弈的奖品；用one grain of rice for the first square，two for the second，four for the third，and then double the amount for each of the rest of the squares，even with all the rice in the country的数词，透露数字的奥秘。

【学习目标】

1. 根据插图和标题，预测故事的发展。

2. 获取梳理故事的基本要素（时间、地点、人物、事件起因、经过、结尾）。

3. 依据关键信息，分析国王和智者的性格和情感变化。

4. 分析作者的写作意图，对故事和人物进行评价。

5. 故事情节续写。

【学情分析】

授课对象为八年级的学生，学生英语基础一般，但对故事类文本很感兴趣；在数学课上学习过指数幂，有学科背景知识。同时学生有一定的信息提取能力。但是推断能力和概括能力有限，分析、评价、创新能力有待提高。

【教学过程】

Step 1: Pre-reading

Predicting

Students predict the story according to the pictures, the title, and the introduction, the following questions may help them:

（1）What's the genre?

（2）Who are the people?

（3）What are they doing?

（4）Where are they?

（5）What was the result of the game?

Purpose: To practice students' reading ability of prediction and activate students' thinking.

Step 2: While-reading

1. Reading to get the basic information of the story

（1）Read and draw a mind map including who, when, where, what, why and how.

（2）Read again and finish the plot using your own words or sentences in the story.

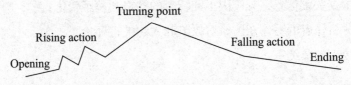

图7-2　The plot of the story

Purpose: To understand the key elements of the story and get the development of the plot clear.

2. Sharing and evaluating

One or two students share their mind map in groups and then in class. Others raise questions or give some advice.

Purpose: To understand more details and modify their own work.

3. Reading to feel what the characters felt.

Read what the characters said and tell the changes of the three characters' feelings.

Purpose: To infer the characters' feelings from the words.

Step 3: Post-reading

1. Role playing

Divide students into different groups and role play the story.

Purpose: To experience the characters and understand the story better.

2. Discussing

（1）How many grains of rice should the king put on the last square?

（2）What do you think of the old man and the king?

（3）If you were the king, what would you do?

（4）Why is the title "The king and the rice"? Can you think of a better title for the story?

Purpose: To practise students' analyzing, evaluating and creating abilities. To infer the writer's intention.

Step 4: Self-assessment

Please tick the sentence if you agree.

※I can predict the story according to the pictures, the introduction and the title.

※I can draw a mind map to get the information：who, when etc.

※I can tell how the story is developed by finishing the plot.

※I can state my opinions on the characters and give my reasons.

※I can analyze the changes of feelings of the king and the old man.

※I can infer what will happen next.

※I can understand the secret of numbers.

Purpose: To enable students to do self-assessment and clearly understand their understanding of the whole article.

Step 5: Homework

Write an ending to the story.

Purpose: To practise students' creating ability.

案例4：Aliens Arrive教学设计

——沪教牛津版八年级下Unit 8 Reading

【语篇研读】

What：

Aliens Arrive是一篇科幻故事，讲述的是地球人的宇宙飞船因故障坠落在一个外星球上而引发的事件。故事是以Tina和Tom姐弟俩的亲身经历展开叙述的，Tina把午夜发现天空中黄色的光，听到噪声等情况告诉Tom

之后，两人开始了探索之旅，他们在森林里看到飞船和外星人，听到他们的交谈。但是，第二天当他们告诉爸爸他们的所见所闻时，爸爸却拒绝相信，但看到Earth这个词时，也陷入了深思。

Why：

通过描述Tina和Tom看到外星人的行为表现以及情绪的变化，设置悬念，让读者了解对地球人眼里的外星人来说，地球人也是"外星人"。进而客观、正确看待外星人，学会换位思考，不要过于担忧。

How：

该文是一篇科幻故事。科幻故事充满奇幻感和戏剧性。文章共10段，分3个部分。第一部分（第1~3段）描述了Tina和Tom谈论自己半夜看到的不寻常事情。第二部分（第4~5段）讲述了Tina和Tom第二天所探寻到的不寻常事物以及当时内心的情绪变化。第三部分（第6~10段）讲述了Tina和Tom告诉他们父母所发现的奇怪生物，但是他们的父亲拒绝相信他们以及当他看到孩子们写出的标记Earth时的疑惑。

作者在文章中，用3张图片形象地向读者展示了故事的主要人物和事件，引导学生能学会通过图片预测故事的情节发展。全文使用一般过去时，以时间为线索，用"at midnight, the next morning, at 6 p.m., the next morning"等，帮助学生梳理文章的故事脉络；通过"heard, mentioned, sure, explore, hid, keep quiet, frightened, discovered, ran away in fear, wonder"等，描述Tina和Tom对于看到奇怪事物的好奇行为与情绪的变化；用"because of"和"since"两个句型，陈述原因。

【学习目标】

1. 通过题目、图片和关键词，预测故事内容。

2. 按时间发展顺序梳理故事情节，并能根据时间轴和关键词以故事中的某一角色复述故事。

3. 能从对话中了解主人公情感变化。

4. 分析推测作者意图，对未知世界持客观的态度。

【学情分析】

本节课授课对象为八年级的学生，在英语知识方面，他们已经积累了一定的词汇量，能独自阅读与其词汇量匹配的文章，并能概括其主要内容。本节课的内容为外星人的相关话题，学生的学习兴趣比较浓厚。本课学习前，学生已经通过听说课了解了与本单元话题——外星人的一点背景知识，这对顺利达成学习目标有很大的帮助。学生有较好的独立思考的习惯，有小组活动的经验，课堂表现积极活跃。

【教学过程】

Step 1: Pre-reading

1. Brainstorming（Questions）

（1）Do you want to travel to another planet? Why?

（2）What might happen if you land on the planet?

（3）What might you do if you meet aliens?

Purpose: To activate students'knowledge.

2. Predicting

（1）What type of text is it according to the title and the pictures?

（2）What questions can you ask?（6 elements:who,when... ）

（3）What might the passage mainly about?

（4）How might the story be organized?

（Teacher writes students' opinions on the blackboard）

Purpose: To develop students' awareness of different genres and their ability of predicting.

Step 2: While-reading

1. Reading for structure and details

Students read the story to answer the questions of predicting.

Teacher encourages students to draw their mind maps while reading.

Purpose: To develop students' logical thinking and analysing ability.

2. Comparing and evaluating

Students compare the answers they get from the story with the results of predicting.

Purpose: To get the structure of the narration and develop a new schema by comparison.

3. Read and answer the question chain

（1）What was the yellow light in the sky?

（2）What happened to the light?

（3）Who are the aliens? How do you know?

（4）Why doesn't the father allow their children to ask?

（5）What are Tina and her family? Why?

（6）Who are the aliens? How do you know?

Purpose: To understand the story deeply and develop their abilities of analysis and inference.

Step 3: Post–reading

Discussing and sharing

（1）What would you do if you were the aliens?

（2）What will happen next?

Purpose: To develop students' critical thinking and to learn to work in groups and share their own problems and solutions with others.

Step 4: Self–assessment

Please tick the sentence if you agree.

※ I can draw a mind map including the main elements of the story: time, place, main characters.

※ I can find out the main plot of the story （beginning, development and ending included）.

※ I can make evaluation and inference about the story.

※ I can apply what I have learnt from this story to retell the story.

※ I can form the idea to be positive to the unknown world.

Purpose: To check whether the goals are achieved or not.

Step 5: Homework

1. Imagine and write what will happen next.

2. Write a short passage about your idea about aliens.

案例5：Archimedes and the golden crown教学设计

——沪教牛津版九年级上Unit 1 Reading

【语篇研读】

What：

Archimedes and the golden crown讲述了国王要求阿基米德帮他检验金皇冠的故事。国王让皇冠工匠给他制作了一顶金皇冠，起初他对皇冠非常满意，但很快就怀疑皇冠不是纯金制作的，于是命令阿基米德检验。阿基米德接到国王的命令后，一筹莫展，在百思不得其解之时，居然在洗澡时突然有了主意，找到了测试"真假王冠"的方法：找两个装满水的罐子，一个放制作好的金皇冠，另一个放同等重量的金子，结果溢出的水不一样，表明工匠在制作金皇冠的过程中掺了假。阿基米德最终揭露了造冠者的阴谋，帮国王解决了难题。

Why：

通过描述阿基米德测试"真假王冠"，作者告诉我们遇到问题要敢于尝试，不断探索，从生活中找方法，培养自己热爱科学的意识。

How：

该文是一篇故事记叙文。记叙文以清晰的时间、地点、人物为线索。文章共9段，分3个部分。第一部分（第1~5段）描述了阿基米德接到国王任务——测试王冠真假后的苦恼和尝试。第二部分（第6~8段）讲述了阿基米德测试王冠真假的过程。第三部分（第9段）讲述了国王得知假王冠后，对造冠者所做的处罚。

作者在文章中，用两张图片生动地向读者展示了阿基米德通过洗澡发现测试方法的喜悦心情和测试时使用的道具。图片的结合有利于让学生意识到生活离实验并不遥远，生活处处皆学问，只要留心观察，认真思索，总会有所发现。"Archimedes was still thinking about this problem as he filled his bath with water"更显示出阿基米德孜孜不倦的探索精神。全文使用对话形式，以王冠测试前、王冠测试中、王冠测试后为线索，帮助学生梳理文章的故事脉络；通过first, next, then，描述了测试的全过程；动词和道具的详细描写，证明这个实验可以被后人操作和检验。通过这一成功的实验，作者旨在告诉读者要勇于探索，不断思考，热爱科学，总会有方法解决难题。

【学习目标】

1. 通过题目、图片，预测故事内容。
2. 画出故事六要素思维导图、梳理故事发展情节。
3. 根据关键词复述检验过程。
4. 分析推测作者意图，培养勇于探索、热爱科学的意识。
5. 通过讨论与同伴合作，完成对故事的口头续写。

【学情分析】

授课对象为九年级的学生，学生英语水平较之前有所提升，特别是词汇积累方面有一定的优势，具备一定的信息提取能力、推断能力和概括能力，同时学生的课堂参与意识较好。但是，在一节40分钟的课堂内，通过教师引导，学生进行思考、讨论、探究，让学生自我提问，还是有一定的挑战性。

【教学过程】

Step 1: Pre-reading

Predicting

Students read the title, pictures and predict:

（1）What is the genre?

（2）What are the main characters?

（3）What is the story about?

Purpose: To activate students' prior schema and to develop students' predicting ability and improve their awareness of different genres.

Step 2: While-reading

1. Reading for the basic elements

Students read the story to get the 6 elements and draw them into a mind map.

Purpose: To develop ss' logical thinking.

2. Reading for the plot and details

Students read the story and finish the tasks:

（1）Draw the development of the plot and share it with others.

（2）Read and answer the questions:

A. Why did King Hiero send the crown to Archimedes?

B. What happened when Archimedes got into the bath?

C. What did the crown maker do to the crown?

D. How did the king's feeling change?

Purpose: To better understand the story and to pay attention to the details and understand the meaning behind the sentences.

Step 3: Post-reading

1. Retell how Archimedes tested the crown according to the pictures and

key words

图7-3 The process of Archimedes testing the crown

2. Discussing

（1）What do you think of the king and crown maker?

（2）Do you want to be a person like Archimedes? Why?

（3）What will happen next? What will you do if you are the King?

Purpose: To help students to practise using the key words to retell and develop their logical thinking and to develop students' evaluating and creating abilities.

Step 4: Self-assessment

Please tick the sentence if you agree.

※ I can predict the story by reading the title and the pictures.

※ I can draw a mind map to understand the story.

※ I can understand the plot by drawing the line and share with others.

※ I can retell the procedure of the test with key words.

※ I can state my opinions clearly and logically, able to persuade others.

※I can give useful suggestions to solve the problems.

Purpose: To check whether the students have mastered the text and practice their self-taught ability.

Step 5: Homework

1. Read the story aloud.

2. Continue writing the story based on the text.

Purpose: To practise what students have learnt in class and cultivate logical ability and critical thinking.

案例6：Two geniuses教学设计

——沪教牛津版九年级上Unit 2 Reading

【语篇研读】

What：

Two geniuses是关于爱因斯坦和他的司机汉斯之间的一则幽默小故事。爱因斯坦经常受邀去各个大学里做讲座。汉斯经常对爱因斯坦说："很开心能载一个像您这样的天才。"有一天爱因斯坦很累，以至于他抱怨不想去演讲，但是又不想让听众失望。这时，汉斯主动提出可以帮爱因斯坦做讲座，因为他已经对爱因斯坦的演讲内容烂熟于心，且没有人认识爱因斯坦。所以他们换了座位。到了学校后，爱因斯坦在听众席听讲座，汉斯则在演讲台毫无困难地讲课，且掌声连连。突然有人提了一个对汉斯来说很难的问题，正当爱因斯坦着急时，汉斯聪明地邀请了"自己的司机"爱因斯坦进行解答。"司机"爱因斯坦完美地解答了难题。最后爱因斯坦对汉斯说："很开心能载一个像您这样的天才。"

Why：

通过描写爱因斯坦与汉斯的故事，让读者明白不仅像爱因斯坦这样的伟人被称为天才、受人尊重，像爱因斯坦的司机这样的小人物也可以被称为天才，受到尊重。通过人物的语言和动作描述，推测和总结人物性格特点；以及学会巧妙地处理突发事件的智慧。

How：

本文是一则故事记叙文。一共8段，分为五个部分。第一部分（第1~3段），故事的背景——爱因斯坦由于不想做演讲，汉斯主动提出帮忙做演讲。第二部分（第4~5段），问题的出现——汉斯顺利地进行了演讲，突然有人提了一个问题，汉斯完全不知道他在讲什么。第三部分（第6段），故事的转折点——汉斯笑着说："这个问题如此简单我的司机都能回答。"于是他邀请"司机"爱因斯坦来解答。第四部分（第7段）问题的解决——爱因斯坦完美地解答了问题。第五部分（第8段）故事的结局——爱因斯坦和汉斯离开了学校，爱因斯坦称赞汉斯是个天才。

作者在文章中分别使用了三幅图片，图一两个人坐在车上，司机在开车，爱因斯坦坐在后座；图二司机在做演讲，爱因斯坦以及其他听众在下面认真听讲；图三还是两个人坐在车上，爱因斯坦在开车，司机坐在后座。

全文使用一般过去时，作者用表示故事时间线的词和短语one evening，at the university，however，before they left，they left the university，a little later展现故事的发展；用动词词组avoid...，let.. down，turned pale，answered the questions perfectly，offered to...描写故事的主要情节；用so many times that...，so difficult that...，such an easy question that... 的表达来形容汉斯听讲座的次数之多，问题之难，问题之简单；用两句"It's a pleasure to drive a genius like you."首尾呼应，不同的说话人，不同的情感，也展现了爱因斯坦的幽默感。

【学习目标】

1. 根据插图和标题，预测故事的发展。

2. 获取梳理故事的基本要素（时间、地点、人物、事件起因、经过、结尾）。

3. 依据关键信息，分析两个人物性格和情感变化。

4. 分析作者意图，对整篇故事及爱因斯坦和他的司机两个人物进行评价。

【学情分析】

授课对象为九年级的学生，学生对故事类文章比较感兴趣，对爱因斯坦有了解；学生有较好的英语基础，有一定的信息提取能力、推断能力和概括能力，课堂参与意识较好。对于学生来说做到能分析和综合运用，表达含有个人价值判断的观点，具有一定的挑战性。

【教学过程】

Step 1: Pre-reading

Predicting

Students read the title and pictures and then predict:

（1）What's the genre?

（2）Who are probably the two geniuses?

（3）Why did they change their seats?

Purpose: To practice students' reading ability of prediction and activate students' thinking.

Step 2: While-reading

1. Reading for the plot

Students read the story and draw mind maps. They can begin with 6 elements or they can draw the plot line and add the 6 elements.

Purpose: To understand the development of the story.

2. Sharing

Students share their mind maps in their groups and then in class.

Teacher finds out students' shining points and encourage them to learn from each other.

Purpose: To do peer learning and to analyze and find out the problems and solutions.

3. Reading for thinking

(1) Why could Hans give the lecture for Einstein?

(2) Why did Einstein turn pale?

(3) How did Hans solve the problems?

Purpose: To develop students'anlylitical abilities.

4. Comparing and evaluating

Compare the main plot with what they predicted and then evaluate their prediction.

Purpose: To form a new schema.

Step 3: Post–reading

1. Role playing

Teacher divides students into different groups and role play the story.

Purpose: To experience and act out the characters.

2. Evaluating

(1) What do you think of Hans and Einstein?

(2) What can you learn from this story?

(3) Why does the sentence "It's a pleasure to drive a genius like you" appears twice in the story?

Purpose: To practise students' ability of analysis and evaluation.

Step 4: Self–assessment

Please tick the sentence if you agree.

※ I can predict the story according to the pictures, the introduction and the title.

※ I can tell how the story is developed by drawing a mind map.

※ I can find out the answers to the questions.

※ I can act out the story with my partners.

※ I can state my opinions on two characters and give my reasons.

Purpose: To enable students to do self-assessment and clearly understand the whole article.

Step 5: Homework

1. Read the story aloud.

2. Surf the internet to find out another humorous story about Einstein or other great minds.

Purpose: To practise students' creative ability.

案例7：What's a balanced diet? 教学设计

——沪教牛津版九年级上Unit 6 Reading

【语篇研读】

What：

What's a balanced diet?是一个关于均衡饮食的对话文本。Doris和Samuel在一家餐馆用餐，两人在点菜时讨论了各自的饮食结构。Doris说自己不吃油炸食品及不喝软饮料的原因——在做完体检后，她听从医生建议，正在减肥和均衡饮食，并引出均衡饮食的含义以及具体的食物种类：大量的水果、蔬菜和谷物类如面条和面包，少吃奶制品、鸡蛋和肉。但Samuel坚持自己的饮食很均衡：早餐，煎蛋和一大杯牛奶甜咖啡，然后还吃点冰激凌作为零食；午餐，吃6个鸡翅和一份可乐，而且每天吃很多种类的食物。Doris评价这些食物都很不健康。最后Samuel表示同意，但却说明天再改善饮食，今天先吃汉堡和巧克力蛋糕！

从文中可看出，Doris对均衡饮食有较好的认知，而Samuel对均衡饮食的认知不够准确，饮食结构不太健康。

Why：

通过描述Doris和Samuel的对话，使读者了解什么是均衡的饮食以及均衡饮食的重要性，同时让读者可以根据食物金字塔评价和反思自己或别人的饮食习惯和膳食结构是否合理，有无需要改进的地方，进一步养成合理的饮食习惯，做到均衡饮食。

How：

本文是对话形式的记叙文。一共30行，可分为三个部分。第一部分（1~10行）Samuel和Doris的晚餐点餐以及Doris饮食改变的原因；第二部分（11~15行）Doris陈述均衡饮食的含义；第三部分（16~30行）Samuel介绍自己的早餐和午餐，以及Doris对Samuel的饮食评价。

作者在文章中分别使用了三张图片，图一是一盘快餐：薯片、汉堡、西红柿、青菜；图二是一盘虾仁炒韭菜；图三是两个人在边吃饭边聊天的情景，Doris 面前是蔬菜、水果、面包和茶，而Samuel面前是汉堡、巧克力蛋糕和可乐。

全文使用了三种时态，在点餐时使用一般将来时，在陈述均衡饮食时使用一般现在时，在谈论医嘱和早午餐使用一般过去时。作者用动词词组 decid to，stay away from，need to，lose a bit of weight，avoid，have a more balanced diet描写关于Doris饮食中需要少吃的东西；用plenty of， fewer， less的量词和such as举例子，说明均衡饮食中每个食物种类的量。

【学习目标】

1.根据插图、标题和简介，预测文章的内容、简单评价两人的饮食。

2.获取均衡饮食的含义。

3. 依据均衡饮食的定义，评价Samuel的饮食，并提出建议。

4. 根据人物的话语，推测Samuel是否会改进饮食，并说明原因或后果，认识到均衡饮食的重要性。

5. 能根据均衡饮食的科学定义，评价和改进设计属于自己的均衡饮食菜单。

【学情分析】

授课对象为初三年级上学期的学生，学生对本话题——饮食，比较感兴趣；学生有较好的英语基础，能做到信息提取、推断和概括，课堂参与意识较好。能积极分享自己的饮食类别，也能对同伴的饮食结构进行评价，但对于学生来说，用英语表达含有个人价值判断的观点，有一定的难度。

【教学过程】

Step 1: Pre-reading

1. Warming-up

Work in groups and finish *What do you know about...*? on P82.

What do you often eat every day?

Purpose: To know different kinds of food and get ready for reading.

2. Predicting

Students predict the passage according to the pictures, the title, and the introduction.

（1）What might the genre be?

（2）Where does the conversation take place?

（3）What are the girl and the boy having for dinner?

（4）What are they probably talking about?

Purpose: To develop students'predicting ability and activate students' prior schema.

Step 2: While-reading

1. Reading and comparing

（1）Skim to get what a balanced diet is.

（2）Scan the text and answer the questions above（in predicting）.

（3）Then compare their answers and their prediction.

Purpose: To check their prediction and form a new schema.

2. Reading and answering

（1）Why does Doris decide to stay away from fried food?

（2）What did Samuel have for breakfast and lunch?

（3）What do Samuel's words probably mean?

（4）If he continues this diet, what might happen?

（5）What suggestions will you give him?

Purpose: To help students understand the text better and develop their critical thinking ability of analysis.

Step 3: Post-reading

Group work & Discussion

（1）Design a menu for our school canteen.

Design a balanced menu→give reasons→introduce your menu→vote for the best one.

（2）Why should we have a balanced diet?

（3）Make a summary on how to be a healthy teenager.

Purpose: To develop students' creative ability, to improve students' thinking ability by sharing and analyzing, to develop their awareness of health care as well.

Step 4: Self-assessment

Please tick the sentence if you agree.

※ I can predict the passage.

※ I can understand what a balanced diet is.

※ I can judge whether Doris's and Samuel's diets are balanced or not.

※ I can state my reasons clearly and reasonably.

※ I can give useful suggestions to make a diet more balanced.

※ I can pay more attention to my diet and my health.

Purpose: To enable students to do self-assessment and clearly understand their understanding of the whole article.

Step 5: Homework

Plan a daily menu for your family.

Purpose: To practise what students have learnt in daily life and cultivate students' ability.

案例8：The great flood教学设计

——沪教牛津版九年级下Unit 4 Reading

【语篇研读】

What：

The great flood是一篇作者描述梦中一场大水灾的虚构故事，是第四单元自然灾难主题中的主阅读。故事讲述了由于地理课上了解了两极冰川融化可能造成的严重后果，故事主人公Kevin梦见自己居住的城市发生了一场特大水灾，通过呈现身边人不同的场景，展示人们因过度关注自己的工作或者娱乐而忽视了这场火灾的故事。爸爸没有时间担心洪水，认为工作最重要；最好的朋友因为玩游戏没时间考虑洪水。最后，到大家受到侵害而不得不注意洪水时，却已来不及。

Why：

作者通过描述Kevin梦中看到水灾发生时的骇人景象以及他和其他人不同的反应，他所做出努力的过程中遭遇的困境，呼吁人们不要过度沉迷于工作或者游戏，要学会正确应对自然灾害，同时树立珍爱生命、保护环境、保卫家园的意识。

How：

该文是一篇记叙故事。记叙文以清晰的时间、地点、人物为线索。文章共9段，分3个部分。第一部分（第1~3段）描述了Kevin做梦前所发生的事情以及做梦的缘由。第二部分（第4~8段）讲述了Kevin梦中水灾发生时的4个不同场景：他在家中、他的父亲在办公室、他的好朋友在家中和水漫城市时人们的不同反应。当然，这些场景中也包括他所付出的努力以及他在这一过程中的情绪变化。第三部分（第9段）讲述了Kevin梦醒时的感受——原来没有发生水灾，这只是一场梦。

作者在文章中，用3张图片形象地向读者展示了故事的主要人物和事件，要引导学生学会通过图片预测故事的情节发展。全文使用一般过去时，以梦前、梦中、梦后为线索，用last week, last night, It was nine o'clock in the morning, very soon等，帮助学生梳理文章的故事脉络；通过looked out of, covered, passed by, were floating, tried to call, sent an email, emailed, shouted, sat, stared at, came into, poured onto, started to notice等，描述Kevin这一场水灾梦，梦中水灾发生时的骇人场景、人们的不同反应以及Kevin的情绪变化；用dreamed about和awoke表达梦中的情景和梦醒后的状况；用I was safe— for now来表达暂时安全的心情和对未来环境的担忧。

【学习目标】

1.通过图片和关键词，预测故事内容。

2.按时间顺序梳理故事情节发展以及主人公的情感变化，理解作者设置的悬念。

3.根据故事情节导图，复述整个故事。

4. 分析推测作者意图，增强珍爱生命、保护环境的信念。

【学情分析】

授课对象为九年级下学期的学生，学生英语水平较高，特别是词汇积累方面有一定的优势，具备一定的信息提取能力、推断能力和概括能力，同时学生的课堂参与意识较好。但是，学生的创造能力和自我提问的能力还有待提高。

【教学过程】

Step 1: Pre–reading

1. Brainstorming

What will you do if there is a flood?

2. Predicting

Read the title and pictures to predict what the story is about and the type of the passage.

In what order was the story written?

Purpose: To activate students' background knowledge and to arouse students' interest on the topic.

Step 2: While–reading

1. Reading for information

Read and get what the story talks about by drawing the plot with key words.

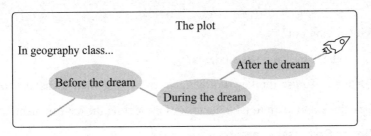

图7-4 Story plot development

2. Sharing and evaluating

Students share the plots they drew in groups and then in class.

After that, students evaluate what they predicted before reading the story.

3. Reading for details

（1）What does "It" mean in the sentence "It started to worry me?"

（2）Why did Kevin have the dream?

（3）How did Kevin feel after Geography class?

（4）How did Kevin feel when he woke up?

（5）Do you think he is still worried about the flood? Why?

Purpose: To form their new reading schema by comparing and to help students to analyze the story and try to understand the purpose behind the sentences.

Step 3: Post-reading

1. Retelling

Students retell the story with the key words in the story according to the plot they drew.

Purpose: To practise their expressing ability and to help students to understand the story better.

2. Discussing

Students try to use the expressions in the text to discuss the following questions:

（1）Do you think such a flood could really take place in our life in the future?

Why or why not?

（2）What can you do as students?

Purpose: To use the key words again to express their ideas and to create what they think and learn to take the task of protecting the environment.

Step 4: Self-assessment

Please tick the sentence if you agree.

※ I can predict the story according to the title and the pictures.

※ I can understand and draw the main plot of the story.

※ I can find out the main elements of the story including time, place, main characters and plot（beginning, development and ending included）.

※ I can make evaluation and inference about the story.

※ I know how to treat natural disasters.

※ I can form the idea that cherish life and protect our home.

Purpose: To help students to regulate and control their own studies.

Step 5: Homework

1. Read the story aloud.

2. Surf the internet and find out how to escape a flood.

Purpose: To cultivate students' problem-solving ability.

第八章　说明文评判性阅读教学案例

案例1：Protect the Earth教学设计

——沪教牛津版七年级上Unit 3 Reading

【语篇研读】

What：

Protect the Earth是一张海报，它介绍了地球上存在的事物。文章先简要说明地球是一个美丽的地方，描述了地球上存在的事物：森林、山川，田地；植物、动物及生活的不同环境；地球上也有人类，地球为人类提供水、空气和食物，是我们的家园。地球上也存在着污染——人类的活动是造成污染的原因，导致了很多动物和植物的死亡。文章在最后呼吁为了我们的未来，我们必须保护地球、停止污染。

Why：

通过描述地球上的事物，让读者了解自己生活的地球的基本情况，警示读者由于人类活动造成了很多的污染，要求我们停止污染、保护地球，同时也引起读者对于如何保护地球的思考。

How：

该文是一张英语海报。海报有6段，分两个部分。第一部分（第1~4段），作者从宏观到微观描述了地球是一个美丽的地方。第二部分（第

5~6段）讲述了人类活动给地球带来的污染，从而呼吁我们停止污染，保护地球。

作者在海报中用四张图片形象地向读者展示了美丽的地球和被污染的现象。全文使用一般现在时，there be 句型结构描述存在的事物，用some...，some...列举了不同天气、动物、居住地等；用burn...to...，put...into...，This pollutes...，and kills...陈述了人类活动给地球造成的危害；用must stop...和It is important for us to...两个句型要求人类停止这些不当行为，呼吁大家为了我们自己的未来而保护地球。

【教学目标】

1. 获取梳理海报的事实性信息（地球上的事物，如山川、河流、动物、植物等；地球目前面临的污染问题）。

2. 梳理归纳文章结构，形成阅读图式。

3. 以环保小卫士的身份，依据关键信息，运用所学到的语言宣传保护地球。

4. 分析推测作者意图，对海报进行评价。

5. 结合个人学习和生活，对作为一名中学生如何保护地球提出自己的建议。

【学情分析】

根据皮亚杰认知发展理论，七年级上学期的学生处于形式运算阶段（12~15岁）的初期，抽象思维开始占优势。英语知识方面，他们已经积累了一定的词汇量，能独自阅读与其词汇量匹配的文章，并能概括其主要内容。本课学习前，学生已经通过听说课了解了与本单元话题——保护地球有关的一点背景知识，这对顺利达成学习目标有很大的帮助，但是学生概括能力还有待提高。学生有较好的独立思考的习惯，有小组活动的经验，课堂表现积极活跃。

【教学过程】

Step 1: Pre-reading

1. Warming up

Students watch the Earth song video and answer two questions.

（1）What is the song about?

（2）What things are there on the Earth?

Purpose: To arouse students' interest and to lead in the topic .

2. Predicting

（1）Ask students what kind of genre this passage is.

（2）Students look at the title as well as the pictures and predict what the poster talks about.

Purpose: To introduce the genre of a poster to get ready for the analysis on the features of poster in post-reading step.

3. Brainstorming

Students brainstorm what they would write about protecting the earth in the poster if they were the writer.（Make an outline）

Purpose: To activate students'previous reading and writing schema about protecting the earth.

Step 2: While-reading

1. Reading for the main idea

Students skim the first sentence of each paragraph and get the main idea of the poster.

Purpose: To develop students' reading skill—skimming.

2. Reading for details

（1）Read the poster and find sentences beginning with"There is/are..."to go with these photos（on PPT）.

（2）Read the poster again and answer the following questions.

A. Where do animals live on the Earth?

B. Why do we need to protect the Earth?

C. What do these things in the last paragraph refer to?

Purpose: To get the specific information and help students find out the language structures: there is/are, some..., some...

3. Reading for structure

Students get the main idea of each paragraph.

Purpose: To get the structure of the poster and get ready for evaluating.

Step 3: Post-reading

1. Comparing and evaluating

（1）Compare their own outline with the poster and judge if they are good writers.

（2）Look through the poster again and tell what a good poster is.

Purpose: To develop students' critical thinking, students can form a new reading & writing schema by comparing their previous schema（written on the blackboard）with the poster's schema.

2. Retelling.

Students work in groups of 4 and make a speech to call on more people to protect the Earth.

Purpose: To help students internalize and apply what they have learned. Giving a speech is to encourage them to role-play in a real context.

3. Discussing and analyzing

Students work in groups and discuss the following two questions:

（1）What's the purpose of the poster?

（2）What do you think of the poster?

（3）What can we do to protect the Earth in our daily life?

Purpose: To help students understand what they should do by inferring the purpose and to stimulate their critical thinking and to enable students to think about their own responsibilities to protect the Earth.

Step 4: Self-assessment

Please tick the sentence if you agree.

※ I can get the specific information about the things on the Earth.

※ I can find out and understand the sentence structures: there is/are, some..., provide...with....

※ I can get the structure of a good poster and use it in my writing.

※ I can give a speech about protecting the Earth according to key words.

※ I understand the importance of protecting the Earth.

※ I know what I should do in my daily life to protect the Earth.

Purpose: To check whether the goals are achieved or not.

Step 5: Homework

1. Read the poster aloud.

2. Search for more information about the Earth and make a poster on protecting the Earth. Remember the features of a good poster.

Purpose: To practise what students have learnt and cultivate students' problem-solving ability.

案例2：Trees in our daily lives教学设计

——沪教牛津版七年级下Unit 4 Reading

【语篇研读】

What：

Trees in our daily lives讲述了树木对空气的作用：保持空气清爽和干

净；吸收空气中的有毒气体，释放氧气，树木是空气污染的主要卫士；树让我们的生活环境变得更加美观；树给我们提供水果、油、茶；木材可以做成家具；但同时人们每年砍伐数百万的树木，所以应该停止砍伐。

Why：

通过介绍树木对改善空气污染的重要作用，以及日常生活中树木的用处，强调树木的重要性，从而结合乱砍滥伐的恶劣影响，呼吁人们应该保护树木，保护我们赖以生存的家园。

How：

本文以对话形式展现树木的重要作用，由Rebecca做采访者，采访Dr. Johns，一共三轮对话，分别从树木对空气污染的有效作用、树木在日常生活中的用处和没有树木的世界三个角度强调树木的重要作用。全文采用一般现在时。

在第一轮对话中，Dr. Johns指出树木能保持空气清新洁净，吸收有害气体，产生氧气以供人类呼吸，有效抑制空气污染。运用一系列动宾短语表达树木的作用：keep the air cool and clean, take in harmful gases, produce oxygen for us to breathe, fight against等。

在第二轮对话中，他们指出树木还便利了人们的生活，可用来制作纸、铅笔等日常生活用品。人们可以从树木中获取水果、油、茶叶等物品。木头可以被用来制成家具。对树的用途做了简单的列举，并运用表示来源或者制作的动词短语：come from, is made of等。

在第三轮对话中，他们强调人们的生活离不开树木的存在，然而滥砍滥伐现象严重，应该加以制止。用双重否定表示肯定：I can't imagine a world without trees. 用动词短语表示人们的行为：cut down, stop doing。

【学习目标】

1. 根据题目、图片、简介预测文章体裁和内容。

2. 运用跳读策略获得文章结构。

3. 寻读文本，查找信息，找出树木的具体作用以及表达方式。

4. 分析与评判树对人类生活的影响。

5. 通过推测与评价，结合现实描述没有树的世界的模样，即毁掉森林，人类将会面临什么后果。

【学情分析】

树木对学生来讲非常常见，但是学生很难用准确的语言表述树木对空气污染的减轻作用以及树木在日常生活中的应用，比如释放氧气、吸收有害气体等等，这正是学习需求可以激发去文章中查询的动力。学生可能在如何保护树木方面，思维有所限制。

【教学过程】

Step 1: Pre-reading

1. Warming-up

Teather shows the picture of a tree to the students and ask them to get to know different parts of a tree: branch, fruit, leaf, root.

Students brainstorm what trees can do for us.

2. Predicting

Students read the title and pictures and predict:

（1）What is the genre?

（2）What does the article talk about?

Purpose: To lead in and get prepared for the topic and to activate students' prior schema about this topic.

Step 2: While-reading

1. Reading for structure

（1）Students read the introduction and skim the article to find out the genre: an expositive type but also an interview.

（2）How many parts can the article be divided into? How do you know that?

Purpose: To grasp the structure of the article and to give evidence when answering questions.

2. Reading for details

Students read and draw mind-maps of the content. And then share in groups and in class.

Purpose: To develop students' own abilities of analyzing.

3. Evaluating

Students and teacher evaluate their prediction.

Purpose: To develop students' critical thinking ability and form a new schema.

4. Reading for language

Students read the interview again and find out how the writer introduce the importance of trees.

Find out the expressions, such as: keep the air cool and clean, take in harmful gases, produce oxygen for us to breathe, fight against etc.

Purpose: To ask students to pay attention to the important expressions.

Step 3: Post-reading

1. Role-playing

Students act as trees to retell the article . (Try to use the expressions in the article)

2. Discussing

(1) What's the purpose of the article?

(2) What the world will look like if there are no trees?What should we do?

Purpose: To develop the ability to express their ideas in many ways.

Step 4: Self-assessment

Please tick the sentence if you agree.

※ I can predict the genre and the content of the article.

※ I can get the structure of the interview.

※ I can find out the importance of trees in our daily lives in 2 aspects and the problem we have with trees.

※ I can find out and understand the sentence structures: keep the air cool etc.

※ I can talk about some consequences of lack of trees.

※ I can infer the purpose of the article.

※ I will protect trees in the future.

Purpose: To check their learning status and achievement of objectives.

Step 5: Homework

1. Read the article aloud.

2. Please write down your suggestions about how we can save trees.

Purpose: By writing down what they discussed about, they can form deeper understandings.

案例3：Great Inventions教学设计

——沪教牛津版八年级上Unit 4 Reading

【语篇研读】

What:

这篇文章讲述了三项重要的发明：车轮、电话和电灯。三种发明用不同的方式展现。介绍车轮时，按时间顺序展现因车轮带来的马车、火车、汽车的出现给人类社会带来的巨大影响。介绍电话时，介绍了发明人、发明时间、对人类的影响、流行程度、作用。介绍电灯时，点明发明人、发明时间，将发明前人们的生活与发明后人们的生活进行对比，突出电灯在人类日常生活中的重要意义。

Why：

通过介绍三项重要发明，让学生了解人类文明发展历程，看似普通的发明可能会改变世界的发展轨迹，车轮是发明车辆必须具备的条件。电话也解决了远距离沟通的问题，电灯更是延长了人类的活动时间。人类文明正是在这一件件发明中飞速发展，不断进步，演变为今天的文明社会。学生通过比较这几种发明的作用和影响，对比形成自己的判断，评估最重要的发明，逐步明确评判标准。

How：

本文是典型的说明文。学生需要了解描写物品的发明人、发明时间、重要影响。文章通过标题"Great Inventions"、三张图片以及引言让学生激活图式，对文章内容进行预测。介绍三种发明的方式逻辑层次不同，使用的语言也不尽相同。文章多次采用表示时间的短语如A few thousand years ago, in the early 19th century，at the start of the 20th century，in 1979，after its invention，since then，before the invention of the light bulb，with light bulbs等等。表示重要性的有allow sb. to do，have been able to do等。学生根据文本查找相关细节信息，了解三个发明的基本信息。通过了解发明物的深远影响，理解人类文明发展的历程。

【教学目标】

1. 根据标题、引言和图片预测文章内容。

2. 通过跳读等获取说明文结构，扫读找到发明的时间、发明人、发展历程、重要影响。

3. 使用目标词汇介绍其中一项发明。

4. 使用表述发展历程和重要影响的短语表达观点。

5. 分析评价文章的结构和内容。

【学情分析】

授课对象为八年级上学期的学生，学生的英语水平为中等，对中国的四大发明比较熟悉，但对于本节课要学到的车轮、电话、灯泡的发明历史只是一知半解，所以存在着信息差。对于说明文的体裁，学生七年级也学过，有一定的知识基础，但相对于故事类体裁来说，学生的兴趣较难激发。如果教师能从学生的某个兴趣点出发进入课文内容，让学生模仿介绍新的发明，定能事半功倍。

【教学过程】

Step 1: Pre-reading

1. Brainstorming

Students brainstorm great inventions they know and tell why they think they are great.

2. Predicting

Students read the title, three pictures and the introduction to predict:

（1）What is the genre?

（2）What does the article talk about?

（3）How might you introduce an invention if you were the writer?

Purpose: To practise students' predicting ability and activate their prior schema and to develop students' awareness of a writer.

Step 2: While-reading

1. Reading for structure

Read the invention "Wheel" and tell what the writer wrote about.

After students find out their answer, they discuss in groups and then teacher asks them to share and give them the right answer.

Purpose: To enable students to pay attention to the content and then understand how the writer describe an invention.

2. Comparing and evaluating

Students compare what they read and what they predicted.

Purpose: To form a new reading and writing schema.

3. Reading for the language

How did the writer describe its history, its development and its influence? （Please find out the sentences and the expressions. ）

Purpose: To pay attention to the language and get prepared for retelling.

4. Reading and raising questions

Students read the inventions（telephone and the light bulb）and raise questions.

Ask and answer in groups and then in class.

Purpose: To develop students'ability of raising questions.

Step 3: Post-reading

1. Retelling

Students choose one of the inventions to retell it to their group members with the words in the artcitle.

Purpose: To better understand the introduction.

2. Discussing

（1）Which of the three inventions is the greatest one? Why?

（2）Do you think the structure of the article is good enough?If not, could you make it better?

Purpose: To develop students' evaluating and creating abilities.

Step 4: Self-assessment

Please tick the sentence if you agree.

※I can predict the genre and the content of the article.

※I can get the structure of describing an invention.

※I can use the expressions I learnt to retell the inventions.

※I can evaluate the structure of an invention and know what is a good structure for it.

※I can understand the importance and influence of inventions.

Purpose: To enable students to do self-assessment and clearly understand if they have achieved their learning objectives.

Step 5: Homework

1. Read the article aloud.

2. Imitate the article and introduce a Chinese invention.

Purpose: To learn to apply what they have learnt and create a new article.

案例4：Fishing with birds教学设计

——沪教牛津版八年级下Unit 3 Reading

【语篇研读】

What：

Fishing with birds是一篇说明文，介绍了鸬鹚捕鱼这项中国劳动人民传承千年的古老技艺。文章先简要介绍了渔民王大民的情况和鸬鹚。又细致描写了王大民用鸬鹚捕鱼的具体过程：傍晚出发，给鸬鹚脖子上系上草，到捕鱼地点，王大民把鸬鹚赶下水捕鱼，天黑之后，挂灯，鸬鹚把鱼带回船舱，王大民把鱼收到筐子里，整个过程不需要渔网。文章最后简述了鸬鹚捕鱼的现状，点明了这一传统技艺后继无人的局面。

Why：

通过介绍鸬鹚捕鱼这项传统技艺，让读者了解这一中国传统文化，加深对祖国传统文化的理解和热爱。

How：

该文是一篇说明文，文章有四个段落，第1段介绍了主人公王大民；第2段介绍了他的捕鱼方式是鸬鹚捕鱼，以及鸬鹚的外表和特长；第3段详细描述了王大民用鸬鹚捕鱼的过程；第4段介绍了在我国鸬鹚捕鱼的历史、现状和未来，帮助读者理解鸬鹚捕鱼这一中国传统技艺，加深读者对中国传统文化的热爱。

全文基本采用一般现在时，文章主体部分作者用大部分篇幅细致生动地描述了鸬鹚捕鱼的过程，运用了表示时间顺序的词汇，如late in the afternoon，at first，then，during the day，after dark；还运用一系列的动词或动词词组，如set off，get... ready，tie，reach，push，use，jump使捕鱼过程非常生动，具有画面感；还使用了被动语态，如are taken，are required等。最后一段用被动语态was practised，转折词（but today），时间顺序词汇（in 50 years），简洁清晰地呈现了鸬鹚捕鱼的曾经、现状和未来，引发读者深思。

【教学目标】

1. 获取梳理鸬鹚捕鱼的事实性信息（如鸬鹚的外表和特长、主人公用鸬鹚捕鱼的过程、鸬鹚捕鱼的历史和现状等）。

2. 梳理归纳文章结构，形成阅读图式。

3. 以王大民的身份，依据关键词，运用所学到的语言复述鸬鹚捕鱼的过程。

4. 结合现实，分析评价作者对鸬鹚捕鱼的未来的看法。

5. 表达自己对保护这种传统技艺的观点。

【学情分析】

授课对象是八年级下学期的学生，学生掌握了一定的词汇量，课堂参与度很高，且有一定的信息提取能力、总结概括能力、评价分析能力。但班级学生英语水平存在差异，因此在设置问题时需要设置有梯度区分的问题，以便班内所有学生都能积极参与课堂。

【教学过程】

Step 1: Pre-reading

1. Lead in

Present some pictures about traditional Chinese skills including cormorant fishing, paper cutting, shadow play, embroidering, Chinese knots and iron forging on the PPT and ask students to match the expressions already given with the pictures.

Purpose: To activate students'prior knowledge about traditional Chinese culture and lead in today's topic and arouse students' interest in reading this article.

2. Predicting

Students skim the title and the pictures to make predictions and answer the following questions.

（1）What is the genre of the article?

（2）What does this article talk about?

Purpose: To activate students' prior knowledge about this topic.

Step 2: While-reading

1. Reading for the main idea

Students skim the first sentence of each paragraph and match each paragraph with their main ideas.

Para.1 What cormorants are like?

Para.2 How the fisherman is fishing with birds?

Para.3 What is Wang Damin?

Para.4 How is the future of Cormorant fishing?

Purpose: To get the structure of the text.

2. Reading for details

（1）What is Wang's job?

（2）What do cormorants look like?

（3）What's special about cormorants?

（4）Read Para.3 and draw a mind-map of Wang Damin's fishing process. （If students have difficulty in drawing the map, they can look at the PPT and just need to fill in the blanks.）

· Time to set off: _____.

· First, Wang Damin _____ to stop ped them from eating big fish.

· Then, after his boat _____ in the river, he _____ and use several ways to _____.

· During the day, _____.

· After dark, _____.

· Finally, the cormorants _____ .Damin _____ into the basket.

（5）What was the past of cormorant fishing?

（6）What might be the future of cormorant fishing?

Purpose: To check whether students can get the specific information after reading.

3. Reading for evaluation

Students quickly read through the whole article again to check whether their prediction about the article is right or not.

Purpose: To check whether students' beginning schema is as good as the article and to improve students' skill of critical thinking through making evaluation while reading and to guide them to pay attention to the writing skills.

4. Reading for analysis

Students read and think about:How did the writer make the process of cormorant fishing so vivid?

Purpose: To pay attention to the way of describing and the verbs that describe the cormorant fishing.

Step 3: Post-reading

1. Retelling

Teacher presents some key words on the PPT and ask students to retell the process of cormorant fishing as Wang Damin.

They can work in pairs: one retells, and the other one acts it out.

Purpose: To experience the vivid words and the traditional skill.

2. Discussing

Students work in groups and discuss the questions:

（1）Do you agree with the author's opinion that "perhaps there will be no more cormorant fishermen in the world"? Why or why not?

（2）How should we treat traditional skills including cormorant fishing?

Purpose: To develop students' ability of critical thinking through asking them to evaluate the author's opinion and to think about what attitude we should have towards traditional skills.

Step 4: Self-assessment

Please tick the sentence if you agree.

※ I can understand the article about cormorant fishing.

※ I can understand the main idea of each paragraph.

※ I can get specific information of the article.

※ I can logically and clearly retell the process of cormorant fishing with some key words.

※ I can evaluate the writer's opinion about the future of cormorant fishing and give my reasons.

※ I can clearly state my own opinion on how we should treat traditional skills.

Purpose: To check whether the objectives are achieved or not and to strengthen students' self-radjusting ability.

Step 5: Homework

1. Read the story aloud.

2. Surf the Internet to learn about more traditional skills and choose one to write an article to describe it, following the writing style of the text.

Purpose: To encourage students to learn more about our traditional culture and to improve their skill of creative thinking.

案例5：How to communicate with your parents教学设计

——沪教牛津版九年级上Unit3 More practice

【语篇研读】

What：

How to communicate with your parents是一篇教孩子如何与父母沟通的说明文。文中介绍了孩子如何与家长沟通的四条建议：一是列出与父母最不能达成一致意见的事情，尽量找到双方都可以接受的结果；二是父母有空的时候，多和他们聊聊；三是要听听父母必须说的话；四是如果没有得到满意的结果，要和父母谈谈，一起找原因。

Why：

通过介绍与父母沟通的方式，引导学生与家庭成员和谐相处，与父母良好沟通，学会换位思考，运用同理心等。

How：

该文是解释事理的说明文，说明文结构清晰。本文以"总—分—总"结构阐释如何与父母沟通。文章共6段，分3个部分。第一部分（第1~3段）引出说明的缘由及对象。第二部分（第4~5段）按照逻辑顺序，介绍与父母有效沟通的方法。第三部分（第6段）通过努力，你能有效地与父母沟通。

作者采用"总—分—总"结构，用first，second，third，finally，帮助学生梳理文章中的主要建议，便于学生快速地定位；通过make，find，require，change，talk，be patient with，listen，understand，try not，learn，live with等，详细列举与父母沟通的建议；用It is no good for you...，Remember that...，How can you expect...? If you don't...，try not to...，Part of growing up is...，learning to understand...等句型，理解说明对象的主要方法。

【学习目标】

1. 通过标题，结合自身经验预测文章内容。
2. 梳理说明文的结构，了解说明文的说明顺序，抓住关键句。
3. 用文章中给出的建议的典型句子表达观点。
4. 分析推测作者意图，学会用沟通方法解决和父母之间的矛盾。
5. 与同伴合作，准确表达自己的观点。

【学情分析】

授课对象是九年级上学期的学生，学生掌握了一定的词汇量，课堂参与度很高，且有一定的信息提取能力、总结概括能力、评价分析能力。九年级的孩子正处于青春期，或多或少存在与父母沟通的问题，这篇文章正好从他们角度出发，教他们如何和父母沟通，因此这个话题对学生来说是"及时雨"。

【教学过程】

Step 1: Pre-reading

1. Brainstorming

（1）Do you have a good relationship with your parents?

（2）What problems do you have with your parents?

（If students can not express their opinions, teacher will show them some pictures to lead to the topic.）

2. Predicting

Look at the title and the first paragraph and predict:

（1）What is the article probably about ?

（2）What will you probably learn from the article?

Purpose: To activate students' background knowledge and prior schema.

Step 2: While-reading

1. Reading for structure

（1）How many parts can we divide?

（2）What's the main idea of each part?

Students read the passage to divide the passage and sum up the main idea of each part.

Purpose: To get the structure of texts of the expositive type.

2. Comparing and evaluating

Compare the structure of the text and the main idea with their prediction. Then evaluate their own structure before reading.

Purpose: To form the new schema by evaluating their prediction.

3. Reading for details

（1）How many suggestions does the writer give?

（2）What must you be ready to do if you want your parents to change?

（3）Why might your parents understand your situation better than you expect?

（4）What is part of growing up according to the writer?

Purpose: To learn to read silently and logically to catch the key information by finishing the question chain.

4. Reading for language

Students read the article again to find out how the writer give them suggestions.

Eg. First, make a list of...

...

Then, they share their sentences with their partners and try to imitate the sentence structures to express their opinions.

Purpose: To help students to think logically and develop their critical thinking and to make students pay attention to the expressions of giving advice and learn to use them.

Step 3: Post–reading

1. Evaluating

Students work in groups and talk about the following questions:

（1）Which way do you think is useful for you? Why?

（2）What is the purpose of the article?

Purpose: To learn to evaluate the writer's ideas and infer the writer's purpose.

2. Discussing

（1）What kind of problem do you have with your parents?

（2）How will you solve them?

Purpose: To encourage students to link their own experience with the ideas and express their own ideas clearly and bravely.

Step 4: Self–assessment

Please tick the sentence if you agree.

※ I can predict what the article is about.

※ I can get the specific suggestions about communicating with our parents.

※ I can get the structure of a good speech and use it in my writing.

※ I can find out and understand the sentence structures: It is no good for you..., Remember that..., If you don't..., try not to....

※ I can evaluate which ways are suitable for me.

※ I know what I should do when I have trouble communicating with my parents.

Purpose: To check if they have achieved their learning objectives.

Step 5: Homework

1. Read the article aloud.

2. Write out your suggestion:

Your parents read your Wechat message secretly. How will you solve this problem?

Purpose: To cultivate students' problem-solving ability.

案例6：The world is in danger教学设计

——沪教牛津版九年级下Unit 3 Reading

【语篇研读】

What：

The world is in danger是一篇说明文，主题是当今世界所面临的环境问题，介绍了致使地球处于危险的三大因素：温室效应、滥伐森林及人们的不良生活习惯，在结尾处给读者提供了一些保护环境的措施。文章首先在引言处指出：我们的地球正处于危险中，我们必须要采取措施保护环境，并点明主题——我们都面临哪些主要的问题呢？文章第一部分（第1~3段）描述了温室效应，第二部分（第4段）是滥伐森林，第三部分（第5段）是人类的坏习惯，第四部分（第6段）中作者提供了一些保护环境的具体做法，并指出，如果我们学着去换种新的方式生活，就可以带来一些改变。文章具有现实意义，描述的问题也能够引起读者的共鸣和警示。

Why：

作者通过描述温室效应、滥伐森林及人们的不良生活习惯这三大导致地球处于危机的因素，使读者了解我们的地球所面临的危机，引起读者的共鸣，唤醒读者保护环境、爱护地球的意识。

How：

该文是一篇说明文，运用一般现在时描述了导致地球处在危机中的三大主要因素。引言部分，作者用We must...警示读者环境保护迫在眉睫，尾句用一个疑问句引出文章说明的主要内容。除引言部分外，文章分为四个部分，前三个部分都有概括性的小标题，即The greenhouse effect，Cutting down trees和Bad habits。第一部分是"温室效应"：首先介绍了大气的功能及其对地球的重要意义，然后说明了温室效应产生的原因，温室效应会导致全球变暖、海平面上升、未来城市可能会消失等后果；第二部分是"滥伐森林"，首先指出滥伐森林的现状，后面说明滥伐森林会产生的后果：加重温室效应、破坏动物家园、导致水土流失及洪涝灾害等；第三部分是"不良习惯"，介绍了人们在日常生活中会导致地球污染的不良习惯，会导致垃圾堆积成山、污染土地和海洋。作者在描述这三大问题时用了cause, destroy, make...worse, result in, create, pollute等一系列表示后果的动词，易于引起读者共鸣，起到警示作用。第四部分，作者运用we need to，we should，we can等句型提供了一些保护环境的措施，结尾句用if条件状语从句告诉读者，如果我们学着去换种新的方式生活，就可以促成一些改变。

【学习目标】

1. 获取梳理这篇文章的事实性信息（如大气的功能及重要性、温室气体产生的原因及其导致的后果、滥伐森林会产生的后果、人类不良习惯有哪些及其后果等）。

2. 梳理归纳文章结构，形成阅读图式。

3. 小组讨论并总结出我们可以通过采取哪些措施保护地球。

4. 提高保护地球的意识。

【学情分析】

授课对象是九年级学生，经过近三年的初中学习，学生已经掌握了较大的词汇量，绝大多数学生能积极参与课堂活动，思维积极活跃，在教师问题的引导下，能够较好地提取信息、合理概括、理性分析评价，但是在理解英文科普知识并在文章基础上拓展思维并进行语言表达上可能存在一定难度。

【教学过程】

Step 1: Pre–reading

1. Lead-in

Students watch a short video clip titled "The planet is in DANGER!!"

What kinds of danger is our Earth in?

Purpose: To attract students' interest in this lesson and lead in today's topic—the world is in danger.

2. Predicting

Skim the title, the introduction part, the sub-headings and the pictures to make predictions and answer the following questions.

（1）What is the article mainly about?

（2）What main problems will the article talk about?

（3）Where might the article taken from?

Purpose: To activate students' prior schema about problems the Earth faces.

Step 2: While–reading

1. Reading for the main idea

Students skim the article and summarize the main idea of the article.

Purpose: To develop students' skill of quickly mastering the main idea of an article.

2. Checking and evaluating

Students check their prediction and evaluate if their prediction is similar to the article.

Purpose: To form a new schema by comparing their prediction with the article.

3. Reading for detailed information

（1）Read and finish the form.

表8-1　The problem impact of the greenhouse effect

Problems	Effects
Greenhouse effect	1. The Earth's temperature increase. …
People's bad habits	1. The greenhouse effect becomes worse. 2. Animals lose homes.

（2）Read the part *the greenhouse effect* and draw a mind map to explain it.

（3）What actions should people do?

Purpose: To find out specific information according to the given questions.

Step 3: Post-reading

1. Inferring

What's the purpose of the article?

2. Discussing

（1）What other problems does the Earth face?

（2）What else can people do to save the Earth out of danger?

Purpose: To cultivate students' ability to make inferences and to further students' sense of protecting the Earth and encourage them to think in a creative and comprehensive way.

Step 4: Self-assessment

Please tick the sentence if you agree.

※ I can find out the main idea of the article.

※ I know the structure of the article.

※ I can realize the three problems that cause the world in danger and know their effects.

※ I can find out how the author states causes and effects.

※ I know what measures we should take to protect our Earth.

※ I am aware that we must take action to protect the Earth.

Purpose: To check their learning objectives are achieved or not.

Step 5: Homework

Surf the internet and find other causes that lead to the world in danger and write a paragraph or an essay to introduce one of the causes.

Purpose: To get students to further find out the causes that put our Earth in danger and enhance their creative thinking.

第九章 议论文评判性阅读教学案例

案例：Pet Dogs教学设计

——沪教牛津版八年级下 Unit 6 Reading

【语篇研读】

What：

这篇文章讲述了Emma和Matt两个人对养宠物的不同观点。Emma认为养宠物是一件好事，因为狗很可爱，在养狗的过程中，养狗人能培养责任心，学会关心他人，也会得到狗无尽的爱与忠诚。Matt认为养狗不是个好主意，会有很多不好的方面，比如打扫卫生非常费劲，狗半夜吠叫影响他人休息，甚至有些狗会咬伤他人，另外，养狗需要很多空间，还会花费很多钱。

Why：

通过对养狗是不是一件好事的辩论，引发对养宠物这个话题的思考，提醒大家养狗需有足够的时间精力和金钱保证，养狗人应根据自己的实际情况做出合理的选择。决定养狗，就要有足够的责任心，爱护宠物，不能半途而废。

How：

本文是典型的议论文，正方和反方都是采用"总—分—总"的结构，进行论述。首先给出论点，然后用事实和观点的论据支撑自己的观点，最后，总结陈述自己的观点。作者在给出论据时，用了First，Second，What's more，finally等衔接词来列举，让读者可以清楚地看到有几条论据。此外，作者还用了It's +adj.+for sb. to do sth. We can learn...from doing sth. Doing sth. can be... 等典型句型论述观点，句型丰富。

【学习目标】

1. 获取议论文写作结构：论点、论据、论证。
2. 学会使用表述观点和论据的过渡词、句型。
3. 了解养狗的好处与坏处。
4. 评价论述过程是否合理。
5. 学会对一个观点表述自己的看法。

【学情分析】

初中阶段议论文较少，学生处于八年级下学期，有一定的语言表述能力，但是缺乏自己产生观点和提供强有力的支撑的能力。通过学习这篇文章，学生应能了解议论文的写作结构和常用表达法，同时，也应该养成对自己的观点要给出合理的证据的习惯。

【教学过程】

Step 1: Pre-reading

1. Lead in

Teacher shows the topic *Head-to-Head* to students and ask them:

（1）What does it mean?

（2）What can you infer from the topic?

2. Predicting

Students read the title, introduction and the pictures to predict:

（1）What is the genre?

（2）What will be talked about?

（3）How will the article be organized?

Purpose: To arouse students' interest in exploring the article and to check if the students know the argumentative type of texts: its structure.

Step 2: While-reading

1. Reading for structure

Students read the first sentence of each paragraph to figure out the structure.

（Idea—Reasons—Conclusion）

Purpose: To get the structure of the argumentative type of the text.

2. Reading for details

Students read and fill in the following form on their worksheet.

Is it a good idea to keep pet dogs?

表9-1　The benefits of keeping a pet

	Emma	Matt
Opinion	Keeping pet dogs is a good idea.	
Reasons/ facts	1.	1. Pet dogs leave their hair...
	2. Second,...	2.
	3.	3.
Supporting details	1. It's nice to hold them...	

After finishing the form, students share their answers in groups. And then teacher will ask one to show and explain his form in class.

Teacher also guides them to understand the differences between opinions and facts. And lead students to understand why supporting details are needed to the reasons.

Purpose: To make the structure clearer and help students better understand the supporting details of each opinion.

3. Reading for language

Students read and find out some good expressions and share with others, such as It's nice to ..., According to...

Students try to use the expressions to express their ideas.

Purpose: To learn how to express their opinions or list facts. Also they can learn how to write supporting details.

Step 3: Post-reading

Evaluating

Students work in groups to discuss:

（1）Whose opinion is more convincing, Emma's or Matt's? Why?

（2）What do you think of their grounds of argument? Can you make them better?

Purpose: To lead students to think critically and logically.

Step 4: Self-assessment

Please tick the sentence if you agree.

※ I can understand the opinions of Emma and Matt.

※ I can understand each supporting detail of every opinion provided by Emma and Matt.

※ I have known how to give my opinions and how to give supporting details.

※ I can state my opinions clearly and logically.

※ I can evaluate their reasons and supporting details.

※ I have known every time I give my opinion, I need to give reasons and details to support my opinion.

Purpose: To check whether their learning objectives are achieved or not.

Step 5: Homework

1. Read the article aloud.

2. Interview your parents whether they want to keep pets? Why?

Purpose: To practise what students have learnt in daily life and cultivate students' problem-solving ability.

第十章　小说故事评判性阅读案例

案例1：Tom Sawyer paints the fence教学设计

——沪教牛津版九年级上Unit 7 Reading

【语篇研读】

What：

Tom Sawyer paints the fence是美国著名幽默大师、小说家马克·吐温所著的小说《汤姆·索亚历险记》中的一个故事"汤姆漆栅栏"的简写版。该故事讲述了汤姆在担心被同伴嘲笑和完不成漆栅栏任务的双重压力下，设计了一个"圈套"，即让伙伴们对这项苦差事产生浓厚兴趣，争相用自己的宝贝来交换漆栅栏的机会，从而不露痕迹地完成了自己的任务，还得到了一堆宝贝。

Why：

通过描述故事主人公汤姆·索亚的"圈套"，展现了主人公的机智，同时也表现了马克·吐温诙谐幽默的语言风格。故事的主人公汤姆·索亚跟现在的学生年龄相似，但主人公面对困难时，用自己的智慧化险为夷，不但借别人之力完成了任务，还收到了意外之喜。故事告诉读者凡事换一种思路和态度，巧用智慧，总会有解决之道。同时，马克·吐温诙谐幽默的语言，又激发了学生对文学的兴趣。

How：

该文是一篇小小说故事，故事以主人公的情绪变化为线索。文章共14段，分3个部分。第一部分（第1~3段）描述了Tom设圈套之前的心情。第二部分（第4~12段）讲述了Tom设圈套过程中的心情变化。第三部分（第13~14段）讲述了Tom设圈套后的心情和收获。

作者在文章中，运用了大量的对话，正话反说，明明是不愿意做，却在小伙伴面前说机会难得，更显示了Tom的幽默和机智以及马克·吐温的幽默，如：

"Do you want to come? Oh,you have to work, don't you? What's a pity!"

"Work?"Tom said. " This isn't work. I'm enjoying myself. Does a boy get a chance to paint a fence like this every day?"

【教学目标】

1. 梳理故事情节：故事发生的时间、地点、人物、过程。

2. 推理主人公的情感变化及性格特征。

3. 找出自己喜欢的句子，并说明理由。

4. 通过角色扮演，理解人物与马克·吐温的幽默。

5. 推测作者意图，评价小说主人公的性格特征。

【学情分析】

授课对象为九年级学生，学生英语水平较之前有所提升，特别是词汇积累方面有一定的优势，具备一定的信息提取能力、推断能力和概括能力，同时学生的课堂参与意识较好。小说类文章是学生第一次接触，与一般记叙文不一样的是，里面有大量的对话，需要他们通过角色扮演来体会小说中的人物和理解人物的心理变化，因此，这节课更需要调动学生积极性，积极参与角色扮演。

【教学过程】

Step 1: Pre-reading

Predicting

Read the introduction and the title of the story and predict:

（1）What is the name of the novel?

（2）Who is the writer of the novel?

（3）What are the boys doing?

（4）Which boy in the picture do you think is Tom Sawyer? What is he doing?

Purpose: To develop students' predicting skill according to the pictures, title and the first paragraph.

Step 2: While-reading

1. Scanning

Students scan the story and find the answers to questions 3&4 in predicting activity.

Purpose: To practise reading for the specific informatiom.

2. Evaluating

Students evaluate what they predicted.

Purpose: To check their prediction and form a new schema.

3. Reading for the six elements

（who, when, where, what, why, how）

Students get the elements and try to raise questions using them. For example:

Who were the characters in the story?

When did the story happen?

...

Purpose: To get to know the basic information of a story.

4. Reading for details

(1) What was Tom's trick?

(2) How did he plan it step by step?

(3) How did his feelings change?

(find out the sentences)

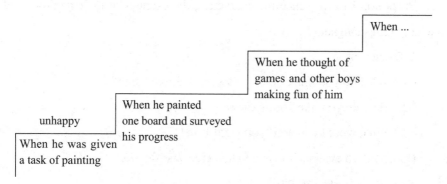

When ...

When he thought of
games and other boys
making fun of him

When he painted
one board and surveyed
his progress

unhappy

When he was given
a task of painting

图 10-1　Reading guidance

Purpose: To get detailed information and analyze the feelings.

5. Reading for language

Students find out the sentences they like and share with others. And they state their reasons.

Purpose: To appreciate the language and get prepared for their writing.

6. Reading for inferring

Students read the following sentences and figure out who said the sentences and what they really meant.

· Work? This isn't work. I'm enjoying myself.

· Will you let me do some painting?

· I'm going swimming. Do you want to come?

· No, Ben, I can't. Aunt Polly warned me to do it well.

· I can do it. I'll be really careful.

· I'm the only person that can do it right.

· I'll give you half my apple. Wait, I'll give you all of it.

Purpose: To develop students' inferring ability.

Step 3: Post–reading

1. Role-playing

Students work in groups and role play the story.

Purpose: To experience the characters, the changes of their feelings, and the humourous language.

2. Discussing

（1）What do you think of Tom Sawyer and Ben Rogers?

（2）How do you like Tom's trick?

（3）What would you do if you were Tom?

Purpose: To evaluate the main characters and the story.

Step 4: Self–assessment

Please tick the sentence if you agree.

※ I can understand the plot of the story.

※ I can find out the 6 elements.

※ I can understand the development of the story and the changes of Tom's feelings.

※ I can find some good sentences and share them with others.

※ I can infer the meanings behind.

※ I can evaluate the characters and the story.

Purpose: To check how much they have learned.

Step 5: Homework

Practise and make the role-play better.

Purpose: To better understand the story.

案例2：The Gifts教学设计

——沪教牛津版九年级上Unit 8 Reading

【语篇研读】

What：

The Gifts讲述了圣诞节前夕，贫困的Della和Jim夫妇为了给对方购买圣诞礼物，卖掉自己最珍贵的物品。Della卖掉了自己瀑布似的长发给Jim买了表链以匹配他祖传的金表，而Jim卖掉了自己的金表换来了与Della美丽的长发相匹配的发梳。双方为了表达自己深切的爱，都舍弃了自己最有价值的物品。

Why：

通过这个感人的爱情故事，让学生感受爱与奉献。真正宝贵的爱情无法用金钱衡量。爱最珍贵之处在于相互关心相互付出。

How：

本文是小说节选，通过行为和细节描写展现夫妻双方的心理活动变化，展现了双方对彼此深刻的爱。比如，通过三次数自己拥有的金钱，One dollar and eighty-seven cents. That was all. Three times Della counted it. 表现Della在节日的热闹中的无力感，家庭一贫如洗，无法拿出多余的钱给丈夫一个惊喜。困苦中似乎看不到希望。又通过Della put on her old brown jacket and her old brown hat. 两次"old"的描述，体现Della穿了多年的旧衣没有钱更换，也舍不得为自己添置新衣，却想方设法为丈夫买礼物。Then Della searched through the stores looking for a present for Jim. She found it at last. It was a watch chain. The bill was twenty-one dollars. 描述了Della历尽

千辛万苦寻找礼物的过程。At seven o'clock, the coffee was made and dinner was ready. Jim was never late. Della heard his steps on the stairs.又展现Della忐忑等待丈夫归来看到礼物的过程。

【学习目标】

1. 获取小说六要素信息。

2. 分析小说矛盾冲突，深入理解小说情节，形成阅读图式。

3. 角色扮演，体会小说人物心理变化。

4. 分析推测作者意图，对小说人物进行评价，体会夫妻之间深刻的爱情和彼此做出的牺牲。

5. 进行角色代入，提供解决方案，并预测后续情节。

【学情分析】

学生到了九年级，已经具备一定的词汇量和阅读能力，对小说类文章有阅读经历，了解了小说要素提取和情节分析的方法，但该篇故事主要通过动作和人的行为塑造人物形象，学生需要学会找到展现人物心理活动变化的描写，并感知人物的心理变化，这对他们来说比较有挑战性。

【教学过程】

Step 1: Pre-reading

Predicting

Read the title and pictures to predict the TPCS（time, place, characters, story）.

Purpose: To get to know the topic and have a general understanding of the elements of a novel.

Step 2: While-reading

1. Reading and checking

Read the whole story quickly and check TPCS.

Purpose: To help students check TPCS and form a new schema.

2. Reading and analyzing

（1）Why did Della cry?

（2）How did Della solve this problem?

（3）Why did Jim fix his eyes on Della and show strange expression?

（4）What did they lose in order to buy gifts for each other?

（5）Read the description of Della's behaviors and figure out how her feelins changed:

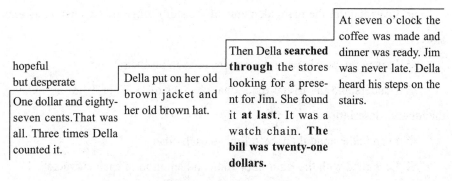

hopeful but desperate

One dollar and eighty-seven cents.That was all. Three times Della counted it.

Della put on her old brown jacket and her old brown hat.

Then Della **searched through** the stores looking for a present for Jim. She found it **at last**. It was a watch chain. **The bill was twenty-one dollars.**

At seven o'clock the coffee was made and dinner was ready. Jim was never late. Della heard his steps on the stairs.

图10-2　Reading guidance

Purpose: To analyze the plots of the story and find out their conflicts and the solutions.

3. Reading for language

Students find out the sentences they like and share with others. And they state their reasons.

Purpose: To pay attention to the detailed description and the emotional changes they conveyed.

Step 3: Post-reading

1. Role-playing

Students work in groups and role play the story.

Purpose: To help students acquire deep understanding of the characters by role-play.

2. Discussing

（1）What do you think of the relationship between Jim and Della?

（2）Would you make the same decision with them if you were one of them?

Purpose: To evaluate the characters and understand the intention of the writer and the story.

Step 4: Self-assessment

Please tick the sentence if you agree.

※ I can acquire the main elements of the story: time, place, characters and story.

※ I know the problems and solutions to each problem.

※ I understand the trivial emotional changes of Della and Jim by reading the relative descriptions.

※ I can understand their deep love to each other.

※ I can read with the right intonation and emotion of each character.

※ I can give my opinions if I were one of them and offer reasons.

Purpose: To check how much they have achieved.

Step 5: Homework

1. Read the story aloud.

2. Write an ongoing story.

Purpose: To practise creating ability.

案例3：The Last Leaf教学设计

——沪教牛津版九年级上Unit 8 More practice

【语篇研读】

What：

The Last Leaf是欧·亨利的短篇小说《最后一片叶子》的简写版。故事讲述了一个生命垂危的病人从房间里看窗外墙上的常青藤叶子在秋风中一片片掉落下来。病人望着萧萧落叶，对生命充满了绝望，她觉得当树叶全部掉光时，她也要死了。但一夜风雨后，最后一片"叶子"始终没有落下来。病人受到鼓舞后，竟奇迹般地活了下来。最后，病人得知，最后一片叶子其实早已落下，是一位老画家画了一片叶脉青翠的树叶在窗外的墙上。而老画家则因淋雨受风寒而去世了。

Why：

通过描述一个简单却感人至深的故事，作者再现了希望的重要性，因为它让垂危病人重燃生活的信心；而希望的给予却是老画家以牺牲自我生命为代价，这展现了为他人牺牲自我的大爱，这份善良体现了人与人之间的美好与温情。

How：

该文是一篇短篇小说。以时间为顺序，文中用了许多表示时间的词语，如开篇交代了故事发生的时间November，接下来很多表示具体时间的词the next morning，at night，a few days later，that afternoon，today让故事情节扣人心弦，一步步引人入胜。作者运用数字six，five，four...last one，形象地写出了Sue对生活希望的一步步破灭，直到消失殆尽。但the last leaf极其渺小的存在，却给了Sue无限的希望。作者开篇先交代时间是November，最后用ice cold，wet all night写出了60多岁的Behrman为了给Sue活下去的希望，做出的巨大牺牲。Behrman不顾自己的身体状况，冒着寒风冷雨画叶子的情形，他画了一整晚，可见难度极大，但他依然选择坚持。

【学习目标】

1. 通过扫读，快速找出小说中的人物、时间、地点等要素。
2. 梳理故事的时间发展顺序，找出Sue的情感变化。
3. 分析推测作者意图，理解作者对希望，人间大爱这种主题的讴歌。
4. 有理由地评价小说中的人物、故事情节。

【学情分析】

授课对象为九年级的学生，学生英语水平较高，特别是词汇积累方面有一定的优势，具备一定的信息提取能力、推断能力和概括能力，同时学生的课堂参与意识较好。对小说类文章的阅读有一定的认识基础，在分析人物心理变化方面稍微欠缺。

【教学过程】

Step 1: Pre-reading

1. Brainstorming

What do you know about O.Henry and his short stories?

Teacher shows a picture and some key information about O.Henry including his real name,the date when he was born, his writing style and so on.

2. Predicting

Students read the title, the picture and answer questions:

（1）What will the story talk about from the title?

（2）What's the color of the leaf? Why?

Purpose: To make students know the background knowledge about the story and the writer and then they can better understand the short story.

Step 2: While-reading

1. Reading and checking

Read the whole story quickly and check TPCS.

Purpose: To get the main idea and the plot.

2. Reading for the plot

Students read the story carefully and draw the plot: the beginning, the development and the ending.

3. Reading for details

(1) Why did Johnsys was going to die?

(2) What made Johnsy decide to live?

(3) What did Behrman do to cost him his life?

(4) What can be used to describe the characteristics of Sue and Behrman?

(5) How did Sue's feelings change?

Purpose: To better understand the story and analyze the story.

Step 3: Post-reading

Evaluating

(1) What do you think of Behrman?

(2) What do you learn from the story?

Purpose: To learn to evaluate the character by finding the evidence from the story and learn to sacrifice.

Step 4: Self-assessment

Please tick the sentence if you agree.

※ I can understand the plot of the story.

※ I can find out the 6 elements.

※ I can understand the development of the story and the changes of Sue's feelings.

※ I can find some good sentences and share them with others.

※ I can know the purpose of the story.

※ I can evaluate the characters and the story.

※ I will love others and the world.

Purpose: To check whether students master what they have learnt and their understanding to the story.

Step 5: Homework

1. Adapt the text into a play and act in groups and present it next class.

2. Surf the internet to find the complete version of the story.

Purpose: To practise what students have learnt in class and cultivate students' interest in literature.

附　录

附录一　调查问卷

亲爱的同学你好!

下面是详判性思维能力在性格上所表现出来的特质。他们当中有些特质可能你是非常赞同的,有些特质可能你是非常不赞同的,请根据你自己的情况来判定它们。

请先仔细看清每一特质,并确信你已经理解了它的含义,然后参看下表,在相应的题号下,按照下面的程度说明,将对应的数字打钩,以表示你对该项目的赞同程度。(1.非常不赞同;2.不太赞同;3.不赞同;4.部分赞同;5.赞同;6.非常赞同)

整个测试过程将持续20~30分钟。当测试用时少于20分钟时,测试结果的准确性将大幅降低,为确保准确的情况,请您耐心答题,谢谢你的配合!

你的姓名:＿＿＿＿＿＿＿

你的年龄:＿＿＿＿＿＿＿

你的班级:＿＿＿＿＿＿＿

题目	非常不赞同 ◄━━► 非常赞同					
1.面对有争议的问题,要从不同的见解中选择其一,是极不容易的	1	2	3	4	5	6
2.对某件事如果有四个理由相同,而只有一个理由反对,我会选择赞同						
3.即使有证据与我的想法不符,我也会坚持我的想法						

续　表

题目	非常不赞同 ←———→ 非常赞同					
4.处理复杂问题时，我感到惊慌失措						
5.当我表达自己的意见时，我感到惊慌失措						
6.我只会寻找一些支持我看法的事实，而不会去找一些反对我看法的事实						
7.有很多问题我会害怕去寻找事实的理由						
8.既然我知道怎样作决定，我便不会反复考虑其他的选择						
9.我不知道应该用什么标准来衡量绝大部分问题						
10.个人的经验是验证真理的唯一标准						
11.了解别人对事物的想法，对我来说是重要的						
12.我正尝试少做主观的判断						
13.研究外国人的想法是很有意义的						
14.当面对困难时，要考虑事件所有的可能性，这对我来说是不可能做到的						
15. 在小组讨论时，若某人的见解被其他人认为是错误的，他便没有权利去表达意见						
16.外国人应该学习我们的文化，而不是要我们去了解他们的文化						
17.他人不应该强逼我去为自己的意见作辩护						
18.对不同的世界观（例如：进化论、有神论）持开放态度，并不是那么重要						
19.个人有权利发表他们的意见，但我不会理会他们						
20.我不会怀疑众人都认为是理所当然的事						
21.当他人只用浅薄的论据去为好的构思护航，我会感到着急						
22.我的信念都必须有依据支持						
23.要反对别人的意见，就要提出理由						

题目	非常不赞同 ◄──► 非常赞同					
24.我发现自己常评估别人的论点						
25.我可以算是个有逻辑的人						
26.处理难题时，首先要弄清楚问题的症结所在						
27.我善于有条理地去处理问题						
28.我并不是一个很有逻辑的人，但却常常装作有逻辑						
29.要知道哪一个是较好的解决方法，是不可能的						
30.生活的经验告诉我，处事不必太有逻辑						
31.我总会先分析问题的重点所在，然后才解答它						
32.我很容易整理自己的思维						
33.我善于策划一个有系统的计划去解决复杂的问题						
34.我经常反复思考在实践和经验中的对与错						
35.我的注意力很容易受到外界环境影响						
36.我可以不断谈论某一问题，但不在乎问题是否得到解决						
37.当我看见新产品的说明书复杂难懂时，我便放弃继续阅读下去						
38.别人说我作决定时过于冲动						
39.别人认为我作决定时犹豫不决						
40.我对争议性话题的意见，大多跟随最后与我谈论的人						
41.我欣赏自己拥有精确的思维能力						
42.需要思考而非全凭记忆作答的测验较适合我						
43.我的好奇心和求知欲受到别人欣赏						

题目	非常不赞同 ←——→ 非常赞同					
44.面对问题时，因为我能做出客观的分析，所以我的同学会找我作决定						
45.对自己能够想出有创意的选择，我很满足						
46.做决定时，其他人期待我去制定适当的准则作指引						
47.我的求知欲很强						
48.对自己能够了解其他人的观点，我很满足						
49.当问题变得棘手时，其他人会期待我继续处理						
50.我害怕在课堂上提问						
51.研究新事物能使我的人生更丰富						
52.当面对一个重要抉择前，我会先尽力搜集一切有关的资料						
53.我期待去面对富有挑战性的事物						
54.解决难题是富有趣味性的						
55.我喜欢去探索事物是如何运作的						
56.无论什么话题，我都渴望知道更多相关的内容						
57.我会尽量去学习每一样东西，即使我不知道它们何时有用						
58.学校里大部分的课程是枯燥无味的，不值得去学						
59.学校里的有些科目是浪费时间的						
60.主动尝试去解决各样的难题，并非那么重要						
61.最好的论点，往往来自对某个问题的瞬间感觉						
62.所谓真相，不外乎个人的看法						
63.付出高的代价（如金钱、时间、精力），便一定能换取更好的意见						

续 表

题目	非常不赞同 ←→ 非常赞同				
64.当我持开放的态度，便不知道什么是真、什么是假					
65.如果可能的话，我会尽量避免阅读					
66.对我自己所相信的事，我是坚信不疑的					
67.用"比喻"去理解问题，像在公路上驾驶小船					
68.解决难题的最好方法是向别人问取答案					
69.事物的本质和它的表象是一致的					
70.有权势的人所作的决定便是正确的决定					

附录二 前测试题

八年级学生前测试题

阅读理解（30%，共20小题，每小题1.5分）

A

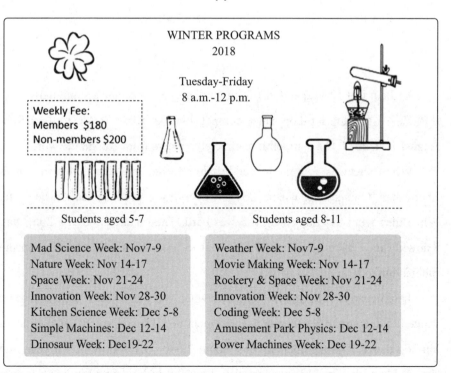

WINTER PROGRAMS
2018

Tuesday-Friday
8 a.m.-12 p.m.

Weekly Fee:
Members $180
Non-members $200

Students aged 5-7

Mad Science Week: Nov7-9
Nature Week: Nov 14-17
Space Week: Nov 21-24
Innovation Week: Nov 28-30
Kitchen Science Week: Dec 5-8
Simple Machines: Dec 12-14
Dinosaur Week: Dec19-22

Students aged 8-11

Weather Week: Nov7-9
Movie Making Week: Nov 14-17
Rockery & Space Week: Nov 21-24
Innovation Week: Nov 28-30
Coding Week: Dec 5-8
Amusement Park Physics: Dec 12-14
Power Machines Week: Dec 19-22

51. Which of these programs can a student aged 10 join in? (　　)

　　A. Weather Week.　　　　　　B. Kitchen Science Week.

　　C. Nature Week.　　　　　　　D. Simple Machines.

52. Which of the following activities is NOT held in December? (　　)

　　A. Coding Week.　　　　　　　B. Amusement Park Physics.

　　C. Movie Making Week.　　　　D. Simple Machines.

53. What program can Andy（aged 7）and Mary（aged 9）join in together? (　　)

　　A. Coding Week.　　　　　　　B. Innovation Week.

　　C. Mad Science Week.　　　　　D. Nature Week.

54. Lucy（a member）and Tommy（a non-member）want to join Dinosaur week. How much should they pay together? (　　)

　　A. $360.　　　　　　　　　　B. $380.

　　C. $400.　　　　　　　　　　D. $560.

B

Xi Jiaqi is a 12-year-old girl from Xinjiang. She became a semifinalist（半决赛选手）at a top hip-hop dance competition *the World Battles* in the US on August 11st, 2017.The competition attracted dancers from around the world.

When she was 7, her mother left her father and decided to move to Zhongshan, Guangdong, where they left everything behind to start a new life. When they went to Zhongshan, life was hard. They had to live in a 20m^2 flat. Knowing they have no money, Jiaqi went to look for bottles to sell from the rubbish bin to help.

Jiaqi began to pick up hip-hop dance when she was 7 years old. Her mother wanted to encourage her to exercise and meet new friends, so she let Jiaqi learn hip-hop dance. The membership cost about 2,000 yuan（US$300）a year, and she could practise two hours every day. Jiaqi fell in love with hip-hop dance at first sight. She showed great interest in hip-hop dance.

Jiaqi started to attend competitions at 9. She was very independent. She has attended many competitions all by herself since she was 9. In July in 2017, She won *China's hip-hop dance competition* in Shanghai. Later, she took part in a top hip-hop dance competition in the US.

While Jiaqi had found something she loved to do, things at home became harder. Her mother was badly ill and she couldn't go to the United States with her daughter. The US trip was Jiaqi's first abroad, she was nervous but also excited.

Jiaqi said, "I'm impressed by dancers from different parts of the world and their high-level dancing during the competition. My primary goal in this trip is to learn as much as I could from every dancer I will meet and battle with."

55. What did Jiaqi do to help the family? (　　)

　　A. Do homework for her classmates.

　　B. Look for bottles to sell from the rubbish bin.

　　C. Ask her relatives to give some money.

　　D. Collect money at a dancing competition.

56. How old was Jiaqi when she started to attend competition? (　　)

　　A.5.　　　　　　　　　　　B. 7.

　　C. 9.　　　　　　　　　　　D. 12.

57. Which of the following is true? (　　)

　　A .Xi Jiaqi was born in Xinjiang in 2005.

　　B. Xi Jiaqi's mother went to the US with her daughter.

　　C. Xi Jiaqi has been to the US for many times since she was 9.

　　D. Xi Jiaqi won *China's hip-hop dance competition* in Zhongshan.

58. Where can we probably find this passage? (　　)

　　A. In a science book.　　　　　B. In a travel guide.

　　C. In an encyclopedia.　　　　 D. In a newspaper.

C

Alan was a thin old man who lived all alone. One day he got a bad cold and he called for a doctor.

While the doctor was examining Alan, he asked, "Don't you have a friend who could come and take care of you?"

"No, I've never had any friends," the old man said.

"You've lived here all your life and never had a friend?" the doctor said with surprise.

"I'm 64 years old, but I've never met anyone I could call a friend," Alan said. "If it isn't one thing wrong with them, it's another."

"Our village head, Robin, will surely help you if he knows you are sick," the doctor said.

"It's so boring to listen to Robin," Alan added. "You'd imagine there was nothing in this world but his wheat field and his wonderful, healthy pigs."

"Then what about Max, who lives down the road?"

"A selfish（自私的）man, though he's smart and interesting to talk to," Alan continued. "He visited me a lot before. But he'd come only when he felt like doing so. I don't call that friendliness. "

"You can't bring us anything against Toby. Everyone loves him," the doctor laughed.

"Right," agreed Alan. "Toby would live on my doorstep（门槛，门口）if I let him. But he's so noisy that I can't stand him for more than five minutes."

"I'm afraid you see so much of your neighbors' weakness that you're blind to what good people they actually are," the doctor said. **"You're a hard nut to crack, old man!** Anyway, please call me if you need me." The doctor left and he did not hear a word of "thank you".

59. The doctor was surprised because Alan _____. (   )

    A. was such a quiet man

B. had a very bad cold

C. didn't have a real friend

D. knew a lot about the village

60. What does the doctor think of Robin? (　　)

A. Boring.   B. Selfish.

C. Noisy.   D. Helpful.

61. What does the **underlined** sentence in the last paragraph mean? (　　)

A. The nuts you bought were hard to open.

B. You are so difficult to get along with.

C. You tried so hard to make friends.

D. You need to see an old doctor.

62. What can we learn from the story? (　　)

A. We should not let the old live alone.

B. We should do exercise every day to keep healthy.

C. Doctors would like to hear "thank you" from patients.

D. We should try to see goodness of people instead of weakness.

D

More and more Chinese students go on overseas study tours during summer holidays.

Study tours usually include language classes, sightseeing and international communication. It totally meets（满足）the needs of Chinese parents and students for a long and fruitful holiday, though the costs are as high as around 4,000 to 6,000 US dollars.

In 2017, the number of students going abroad for study tours grows by nearly 40 percent, according to English First, a Swedish-English education company in China.

A recent report showed that most study tourists were teenagers in middle school. It was also reported that 73% of the tourists in 2016 were middle school students, 11% primary school students and only 3% college students.

Study tourists in other countries are at least 13 or 14 years old, while Chinese parents seem to be more willing to let their children go on tours at a very young age. One of the tourists Chiu said that the youngest Chinese student on his program was only 5 years old.

Many parents said that going on a study tour does not lead to going to a foreign university in the future. They said that they preferred their child to go to a top Chinese university instead. Some parents think staying in China is a better choice for their children, and such overseas study tours are more about knowledge which children cannot learn from textbooks.

63. When do most Chinese students go on overseas study tours? (   )

    A. During the Chinese New Year.

    B. During the summer holiday.

    C. During the winter vocation.

    D. During Christmas.

64. Why do so many students take part in overseas study tours? (   )

    A. Because the costs are not very high.

    B. Because foreign countries are more beautiful.

    C. Because they want to have a meaningful holiday.

    D. Because they want to go to a foreign university.

65. Who likes to take overseas study tours best according to the recent report? (   )

    A. Primary school students.

    B. Middle school students.

    C. High school students.

    D. College students.

66. What does the passage mainly talk about? (　　)

A. How to choose a good university.

B. The importance of studying abroad.

C. The popularity of overseas study tours.

D. How to improve children's language skills.

E

Imagine you walk into a store. Surprisingly enough, you see no seller inside. You pick up things and prepare to wait in line and pay. But even more **oddly**, there is no cashier（收银员）at all. So what has happened to this store?

Well, you may have entered Tao Café, a cashless store created by Alibaba. In July, people got to see the store for the first time at Alibaba's Taobao Maker Festival in Hangzhou.

The 200-square–meter store sells drinks, fast food and snacks. It can hold about 50 shoppers at a time. To enter and shop, people only need a smartphone with a Taobao App and an Alipay account（账户）.

When shoppers scan（扫描）their Taobao QR code（二维码）, cameras follow them to recognize（识别）their faces. The store has also "remembered" all goods and where they are on the shelves. So when shoppers pick up goods, the system will be able to "watch" and "remember" what they choose.

When shoppers are ready to leave, they don't wait in line to pay. Instead, they go through two checkout doors. Then they will pay with a Taobao account connected to Alipay.

According to Alibaba, the checkout machines can recognize goods even when shoppers put them in pockets or bags. So it is almost impossible to take any things away without paying.

Tao Café is not the only cashless store in China. A 24-hour convenience store with no sellers called Bingo Box opened in Shanghai in June. To enter the store, shoppers scan a QR code on WeChat or Alipay. But unlike the Tao Café, they have to scan another QR code to leave the Bingo Box.

67. What does the underlined word "oddly" mean? （　　）

　　　A. importantly

　　　B. surprisingly

　　　C. interestingly

　　　D. luckily

68. What is Tao Café? （　　）

　　　A. A coffee shop.

　　　B. An online store.

　　　C. A cashless shop.

　　　D. A camera store.

69. If you want to go shopping at a Tao Café, you should have the following things EXCEPT _____. （　　）

　　　A. A smartphone

　　　B. A Taobao App

　　　C. WeChat

　　　D. An Alipay account

70. What can you infer（推断）from the article? （　　）

　　　A. Lots of things will be lost in Tao Café.

　　　B. It saves people much time to shop at Tao Café.

　　　C. We should wait in line when we leave cashless stores.

　　　D. Shopping at BingoBox is more convenient than at Tao Café.

七年级学生前测试题

阅读理解（20%，共20小题，每小题1分）

A

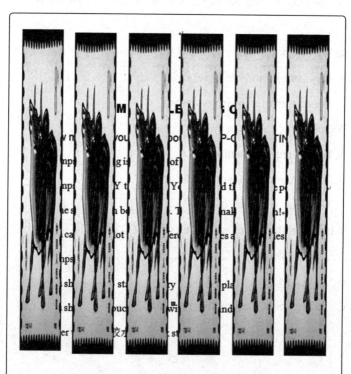

Want to know more about STAMP-COLLECTING?
Join us now!
MOVIEs, LECTUREs and MAGAZINEs
on STAMPs are waiting for you!

56. What can this be? （　　　）

    A. A story.

    B. A poster.

    C. A stamp.

57. Who would like to collect stamps? （　　　）

    A. The young.

    B. The old.

    C. From the young to the old.

58. According to the passage, which of the following is TRUE about stamps? （　　　）

    A. We can find stamps here and there.

    B. Buy stamps and we'll get rich.

    C. We can learn a lot from stamps.

59. Which is the correct way to keep stamps? （　　　）

    A. Keep them clean and dry.

    B. Touch them with wet hands.

    C. Use glue when necessary.

60. What does the writer want the readers to do? （　　　）

    A. To join the Stamp Collecting Club.

    B. To keep stamps at a right place.

    C. To buy some stamps from his club.

B

If someone asks me, "Do you like music?" I am sure I will answer him or her, "Of course, I do." Because I think music is an important part of our lives.

Different people have different ideas about music. For me, I like rock music because it's so exciting. And my favorite rock band （乐队）, the "Fox Ladies", is one of the most famous rock bands in the world. I also like pop music. My classmate Li Lan loves dance music, because she enjoys dancing. My best friend, Jane, likes jazz music. She thinks jazz is really cool.

"I like dance music and rock very much," says my brother, "because they are amazing."

But my mother thinks rock is noisy. "I like some relaxing music," she says. I think that is why she likes country music.

61. What does the writer think of music in life? (   )

    A. Different.

    B. Useless.

    C. Important.

62. What kind of music does the writer like? (   )

    A. Jazz and country music.

    B. Rock and dance music.

    C. Rock and pop music.

63. Who likes dancing? (   )

    A. The writer.

    B. Li Lan.

    C. Jane.

64. What does Mother think of country music? (   )

    A. Amazing.

    B. Noisy.

    C. Relaxing.

65. How many people's ideas about music are talked about in this passage?

(   )

    A. Three.

    B. Four.

    C. Five.

C

There was a pilot（飞行员）and four people in a small plane. Suddenly there was something wrong with the plane. It began to fall down. The pilot told the people there were only four parachutes. They all became worried and started to make excuses（借口）.

"I must go," said the pilot, taking one of the parachutes and jumped out.

The second person stood up. "I'm a doctor," he said, "I help people live longer and I save lives." He took a parachute and jumped out.

The third person said, "I must have a parachute. I am a very clever person and I have to take part in an important match." He picked up a pack and jumped out.

Two men were left—an old businessman and a young mountain climber. At this time the plane was going down fast. The businessman said, "Young man, I am old but you are still young. You take the last parachute." The young mountain climber smiled. "Don't worry," he said. "We can both jump out because there are still two parachutes. Just now the clever man jumped out with my backpack."

66. What does ***parachute*** mean in Chinese?（   ）

    A. 防弹衣

    B. 降落伞

    C.滑翔机

67. What was the second man's reason for having a parachute?（   ）

    A. Saving people's lives.

    B. Going to a match.

    C. Being a young man.

68. What did the clever man jumped out with?（   ）

    A. A parachute.

    B. A backpack.

    C. Two parachutes.

69. Who didn't think of himself but others? (　　)

　　A. The pilot.

　　B. The clever man.

　　C. The businessman.

70. Which of the following is NOT true according to the story? (　　)

　　A. There was something wrong with the plane.

　　B. There were enough parachutes for everyone.

　　C. The businessman and the climber were saved at last.

D

Saving the Earth shouldn't be so difficult if we start by doing something simple.

First, **take our time**. There is no need to hurry. We can walk or ride a bike to work. This is also a good way to avoid（避免）traffic jams.

Second, smell the Earth. Open the windows. Turn off the air-conditioner （空调）, and at the same time, save the energy.

Third, enjoy cooking at home. How nice it is to sit around the table with your family and enjoy the delicious food! What's more, we should use our porcelain（瓷制的）bowls, not the plastic ones.

Fourth, go to the parks near your home. It's always relaxing to spend our weekends and holidays in the warm and comfortable sunshine. Walk into the park, play some games, or just ride a bike around.

Fifth, reuse the old things. Do you agree that it is lovely to pick up the old things that we have almost forgotten? It may take you back to your happy memories. Most importantly, there will be less rubbish if everyone follows this rule. Try to find some in the garden or in the kitchen.

Lastly, no one can build up green mountains or make up clean rivers, but we can protect them. So, remember not to throw rubbish here and there.

71. What does the writer think of saving the Earth? (   )

    A. Impossible.

    B. Difficult.

    C. Simple.

72. What do the underlined words "*take our time*" mean? (   )

    A. Be slow.

    B. Be happy.

    C. Be fast.

73. Why does the writer suggest eating at home? (   )

    A. To enjoy more delicious food.

    B. To avoid using plastic bowls.

    C. To stay in air-conditioned rooms.

74. Which of the following is helpful to protect the Earth? (   )

    A. Drive to work.

    B. Build up mountains.

    C. Use old things again.

75. What can we know from the passage? (   )

    A. Everyone should love their family.

    B. Earth protection can be done in daily life.

    C. Porcelain bowls looks better than plastic ones.

附录三　后测试题

八年级学生后测试题

阅读理解（30%，共20小题，每小题1.5分）

A

VOLUNTEERS NEEDED

at the BHI Museum

Become part of our friendly new front of house team.

We are looking for outgoing volunteers to welcome visitors and help as room guides. The Museum will be opening its doors for the first time this summer, every Friday, between 26 May and 8 September, for visitors to enjoy the museum's amazing collection of clocks, watches and timepieces and we need your help.

Don't worry if you don't know much about clocks and watches. You will be provided practical training and useful volunteer resources, so as to help you get started. We are based in the village of Upton, between Newark and Southwell in Nottinghamshire. The museum depends on volunteers, and if you can spare sometime to help, we would be pleased to hear from you.

To find out more and for an informal chat please call Eleanor Baumber Museum Manager on 01636 817 601 or email bhimuseum@bhi.co.uk

MEET NEW PEOPLE. LEARN NEW THINGS.

SHARE YOUR SKILLS. HELP YOUR MUSEUM.

31. According to the Ad, the volunteers should _____. (   )

    A. be friendly and enjoy meeting people

    B. have great interest in museums

    C. know clocks and watches well

    D. be outgoing visitors

32. What can be part of the volunteers' work? (   )

    A. Collecting the clocks.

    B. Guiding the visitors.

    C. Working as trainers.

    C. Cleaning the rooms.

33. If you want to visit the museum, what time should you go? (   )

    A. Fridays in July.

    B. Weekdays in September.

    C. Weekends in May.

    D. Every Friday of the year.

34. What can we infer（推断）about BHI? (   )

    A. It is not open in the evening.

    B. Visitors are asked to offer help.

    C. It is a small museum in England.

    D. The manager himself is a volunteer.

B

Are you an internet shopper? If you say "yes" then you must know Ma Yun（Jack Ma）, who founded the company Alibaba. Now, he has become one of the richest men in China.

Born in 1964 in Hangzhou, Zhejiang, Ma grew up as a happy kid. When he was a teenager, he wanted to learn English. Every morning, he got up at 5 a.m., rode his bike for 40 minutes to a hotel near the West Lake and communicated with foreign tourists in English. He did it for nine years, rain or shine. The experience made him an excellent English teacher and also opened his eyes to the outside world.

In 1994, Ma Yun heard about the Internet. And on a 1995 trip to the US, Ma was shown the Internet for the first time. He searched the word "beer" on Yahoo, and found that there was nothing there about China. Seeing the chance, Ma returned to China and set up a website called China Pages without even knowing much about computers.

Four years later, Ma, his wife and his friends set up Alibaba in Hangzhou. He believed in the Internet business potential（潜力）when few other Chinese did. Fifteen years later, Alibaba has developed into the world's largest e-commerce company（电子商务公司）, owning popular shopping websites like Taobao and Tmall. With great effort, Alibaba went public（上市）on Sept. 19th, 2014 and raised 25 billion dollars.

Ma's favorite line has been printed on Alibaba's T-shirts. It reads: "Dream still have to have, in case it is realized."

35. What did Ma Yun do to improve his English? （   ）

    A. Took a trip to the US.

    B. Learnt on the Internet.

    C. Worked as an English teacher.

    D. Talked with foreigners.

36. What made Ma Yun set up China Pages website? （   ）

    A. The website was a preparation for Alibaba.

    B. Foreigner didn't know much about China.

    C. He wanted to create it for English learners.

    D. His childhood dream was to get rich.

37. According to the passage, what do we know about Alibaba? （   ）

    A. It was the first e-commerce company in China.

B. It is the biggest e-commerce company on Earth.

C. It sold beers on the Internet at first.

D. Ma Yun started the company alone.

38. What does the passage mainly tell us? (　　)

A. Learning English is helpful for e-commerce.

B. The development of internet shopping.

C. Ma Yun's dream leads to his success.

D. Alibaba raised 25 billion dollars.

C

A woman was at an airport waiting for her flight. She still had a lot of time, so she bought a book and a bag of cookies in the shop, then found a seat to read her book.

While reading, she seemed to see a man next to her took a cookie from the bag in between. With each cookie she took, he took one too. She tried to ignore （忽略）it, because she didn't want to be mad at him. But he kept eating the cookies until there was just one left. With a smile on his face, and a nervous laugh, he took the last cookie, broke it in half and gave one half to her.

"How can this man **have the nerve** to steal all of my cookies and then offer half a cookie in return?" the woman thought to herself. She angrily took the half-cookie out of his hand and ate it without looking at him.

It was time for her to get on the plane. She took all her things and headed for the gate, refusing to look back at the man. After she got seated, she began to look for her book. As she opened her bag, she found in surprise that there was her bag of cookies exactly in front of her eyes.

In fact, the man had been eating his own cookies the whole time and simply wanted to share the last one with her. Finally, she realized that she was the rude one. She really wanted to apologize to the man at that moment.

39. Why did the woman ignore the man's behaviour? （　　）

　　A. To keep away from trouble.

　　B. To let the man eat more cookies.

　　C. To wait until the police came.

　　D. To eat up the cookies before flying.

40. What does the underlined words "**have the nerve**" mean? （　　）

　　A. 吝啬

　　B. 慷慨

　　C. 厚颜

　　D. 焦虑

41. What did the woman realize when she got seated on the plane? （　　）

　　A. She left her book at the airport.

　　B. She ate the man's cookies.

　　C. The man went to a wrong plane.

　　D. The man returned her a bag of cookies.

42. What can we learn from the story? （　　）

　　A. Never share anything with strangers.

　　B. Don't judge others by their appearance.

　　C. Carelessness may lead to misunderstanding.

　　D. Eating cookies in the airport may cause trouble.

D

The Lantern Festival falls on the 15th of the first month of the lunar calendar（阴历）. This day is always the first full moon in the new year. Ancient people also called it Shangyuan Festival. Celebrations and traditions on this day began from the Han Dynasty（朝代）and became popular in the Tang Dynasty.

Watching the colorful lanterns is one of the main traditions. Lanterns of different shapes and sizes are usually put on trees, or along river banks on show. It is said that sky lanterns were first used by Zhuge Kongming to ask for help when he was in trouble. Today, when the lanterns slowly rise into the air, people make wishes.

Another tradition is to eat sweet dumplings. In northern China, they are called yuanxiao while in southern part they're named tangyuan. Because making sweet dumplings is like a game or an activity, they are usually done happily by a group of friends or family members.

One more important tradition is guessing lantern riddles（灯谜）. The riddles are usually short, wise, and sometimes humorous. The answer to a riddle can be a Chinese character, a famous person's name, or a place name. Both the old and the young enjoy the activity.

In old times, the Lantern Festival was also romantic（浪漫的）. Watching lanterns gave young people a chance to meet each other. A line from Xin Qiji, a poet during the Song Dynasty, shows this:

Hundreds and thousands of times I searched for her in the crowd. Suddenly I turned, and there she stood, in the dim（昏暗的）light.

43. When did ancient people start to celebrate the Lantern Festival? （　　　）

　　A. The Shang Dynasty.

　　B. The Han Dynasty.

　　C. The Tang Dynasty.

　　D. The Song Dynasty.

44. What is the second paragraph mainly about? （　　　）

　　A. The history of flying lanterns.

　　B. The meaning of showing lanterns.

　　C. The way of making lanterns.

　　D. The tradition of watching lanterns.

45. From the passage, what can we learn from the traditions of the Lantern

Festival? (　　)

  A. Traditional lanterns are round and red.

  B. The festival was started to make wishes.

  C. Riddles were set to teach children in old times.

  D. The festival was an important day for young people.

46. Why was the Lantern Festival thought to be romantic in old times? (　　)

  A. Because young people could meet each other.

  B. Because it was a chance to express feelings.

  C. Because people could enjoy beautiful lanterns.

  D. Because the activities were funny and popular.

E

  Have you heard of 5G? It is the fifth generation（代）of mobile network technology. These new networks are just around the corner.

  Each mobile network generation is faster and more powerful than the one before it. 1G let us talk to each other. 2G let us send messages. 3G gave us data（数据）and the internet. And 4G made all of these things faster. What's special about 5G?

  About 100 times faster than 4G networks, 5G will let people download and upload data faster than ever before. But 5G won't just bring faster mobile internet. People can use it for many other things as well.

  For example, 5G will help to make self-driving cars safer. Today's self-driving test cars have one problem – delay（延迟）. When the car "sees" an obstacle（障碍物）, it sends this information to a data center and waits for instructions. However, a car accident may take place if the car doesn't receive instructions in time. 5G networks would reduce the time this takes and make the cars safer.

  Because of this increase in speed, it will be possible to create and use new kinds of technology. Doctors in different cities can use robots to operate on patients without any delay.

5G also makes the internet of things（IoT）possible. IoT refers to a large online network that connects all things and people. Smart homes are part of it. For example, with IoT, your fridge could order eggs online itself when it finds that there are no eggs left inside. And you can operate your air conditioner on the smart phone before returning home.

47. What is special about 5G?（   ）

    A. Smart phones become smaller.

    B. It makes a phone call possible.

    C. It is much faster and more powerful.

    D. People surf the Internet with Smart phones.

48. What does "it" refer to in Paragraph 4?（   ）

    A. 5G networks.

    B. The car.

    C. The obstacle.

    D. The robots.

49. According to the passage, which one could be possible with 5G?（   ）

    A. Delicious food is ready when you get home.

    B. Doctors do operations on self-driving cars.

    C. People do not go to the cinemas.

    D. There are no more car accidents.

50. What is the best title of the passage?（   ）

    A. 5G Smartphones Are Coming!

    B. How will 5G Change Our Life?

    C. IoT Technology Is Invented Recently

    D How Can We Live without Smart phones?

七年级学生后测试题

阅读理解（30分）

阅读下面短文，从下面每小题的A、B、C、D四个选项中选出最佳选项，并在答题卡将相应的字母编号涂黑。（共20小题，每小题1.5分）

A

Summer Activities

Science Museum (SCM) Description: You can experience video arts and computer technology, play VR games to explore a future city, and ask the robots questions about science. It will be wonderful! Have fun! Time: July 21st -July 22nd Tel: 21005608	WWI Battlefields and Paris (WBP) Description: You will fly to London from Hong Kong on Day 1. Then travel around London on Day 2. And visit the World War I battlefields in northern France on Day 3. Next, go to Disney Paris park. On Day 5, you will visit central Paris and tour the main sights. You'll have a good time and come back on the last day. Time: August 1st-August 6th Tel: 26241234

续 表

Crafty Foxes (CRF)	Outdoor Adventure (OUT)
Description: Two days of product design. Make lovely things like bags and decorations with recycled materials（材料）. If you are interested in learning skills and making things without modern materials, make a call to us! Time: August 9th-August 10th Tel: 88201593 	Description: Meet new people and learn new skills. You are going to take part in a number of <u>thrilling</u> activities from wild camping to rock climbing. You will also learn to work as a team and enjoy the great outdoor environment. If you are brave enough and want to try something new and exciting, join us now! Time: August 20th-August 24th Tel: 83948695 

26. If you have time only in July, which activity can you take part in? (　　)

   A. SCM.

   B. WBP.

   C. CRF.

   D. OUT.

27. Which number can you phone to get more information about WBP? (　　)

   A. 21005608.

   B. 26241234.

   C. 88201593.

   D. 83948695.

28. What can you do if you take part in CRF? (　　)

   A. Play VR games.

   B. Visit Disney Paris park.

   C. Make things with recycled materials.

D. Enjoy the great outdoor environment.

29. What does the underlined word "thrilling" mean in Chinese? (　　)

A. 流行的

B. 刺激的

C. 舒缓的

D. 创新的

B

As a small boy, Andrew was pretty smart. He was interested in different things. He liked doing things in a way that he thought to be clever. But sometimes he made wrong choices.

One day, his father gave him some money and asked him to buy some goldfish. When he got to the market, he found that the killifish looked like small goldfish, and they were much cheaper. So he bought some killifish and kept the rest of the money for himself.

When he got home, his father realized what Andrew did at once. He put the fish in the tank without saying anything first. He knew his son didn't buy the right fish. At the same time, he thought his son might have an advantage in marketing（市场销售）. And he should think of a way to help his son grow well. He had an idea. Then he said to his son, "Andrew, do you know what you have bought? Are they goldfish?" Andrew felt shy and said in a low voice, "Er, no, but..." His father continued, "Well, I'm glad you know how to save money. I also know you are good at watching things around you. But it's not right to be dishonest. You should do things honestly, or others won't trust you." Then he helped Andrew start with some chores（琐事）like buying daily things, managing his own pocket money and helping his uncle in his store. Later, Andrew worked as a salesman. He felt himself strong in marketing and kept working hard at it. Finally, he became a successful businessman.

Several years later, when talking about the key to his success, Andrew said, "Thanks to my father, I got to know myself well and developed in a right way."

30. Why did Andrew buy the killifish instead of goldfish? （ ）

   A. To save money for himself.

   B. To give his father a surprise.

   C. Because killifish looked more beautiful.

   D. Because there was only killifish in the market.

31. What did Andrew's father do when he knew the truth? （ ）

   A. He kept silent all day long.

   B. He told Andrew to return the money.

   C. He tried to lead Andrew to business.

   D. He got angry and shouted at Andrew.

32. Which of the following words can describe Andrew's father best? （ ）

   A. Rich.

   B. Wise.

   C. Honest.

   D. Shy.

33. What's the main idea of the story? （ ）

   A. Killifish is much cheaper than goldfish.

   B. Never give up and you'll be successful.

   C. It's not right for children to be dishonest.

   D. It's important to educate children properly.

C

Italian architect Micoli still remembers how lonely and stressful she felt when she first moved to Shenzhen. When she realized that she could help the newly arrived Italians in Shenzhen, she didn't hesitate for a moment.

"Doing volunteer work brings me happiness, satisfaction and friendship.

Though I'm busy with my work, I enjoy doing it in my limited free time. I introduce Shenzhen's history and tell them the best places to fix some problems," said Micoli. "The community organizes dinners and lunches for people to talk face to face."

Thanks to her help, many members of the Italian community in Shenzhen have settled down and gotten used to the life here over the past seven years.

Two years ago, three volunteers set up a free website Italian in Shenzhen. com to help the Italians who will come to Shenzhen get some basic information about the city. When Italians reach Shenzhen, they can join a dedicated（专用的）WeChat group where they can find any help they may need.

Micoli studied in Spain as an exchange student during her college years. Before living in Shenzhen, Micoli lived and worked in a number of different cities. "I've got chances to look at my culture from different perspectives（角度）. I've also learned to accept different ways of thinking and found ways to improve myself in the process.For example, Chinese don't like to get dark, so when we design swimming pools, we use shading and add lighting. It's different from Italians who enjoy outdoor swimming," said Micoli, who designs luxury hotels and resorts.

34. What is probably the main reason for Micoli's being a volunteer? （   ）

    A. To help the helpless new comers.

    B. Many Italians come to Shenzhen.

    C. She knows Shenzhen's history well.

    D. She wants to make new friends.

35. What didn't the volunteers do to help Italians in Shenzhen? （   ）

    A. Create a WeChat group.

    B. Teach them to speak Chinese.

    C. Guide them to deal with problems.

    D. Organize activities for communication.

36. According to the passage, Micoli _____. (   )

    A. works as a computer engineer

    B. always feels stressful and lonely

    C. has a lot of free time

    D. is a warm-hearted person

37. What does Micoli think is important when staying in a foreign country? (   )

    A. To accept the cultural differences.

    B. To visit different places of interest.

    C. To make friends with local people.

    D. To design luxury hotels and resorts.

D

An online survey by ride-hailing company Didi found that more than half of the participants agree to allow teenagers under 18 to ride in Didi cars without an adult.

Of the 651,856 people who took part in the survey, 56% felt that those under 18 should be able to hail rides alone. They believe that a safer ride lies more in stricter management of drivers rather than put restrictions（限制）on a passenger's age.

However, some argued that no matter how excellent any safety measures are, they cannot completely stop crimes（犯罪）. They also felt that guardians like parents should be responsible for children who have a weak sense of safety and self-protection.

According to a report in 2018, crime rates for internet ride-hailing drivers are 0.48 per 100,000 people, compared with the rates for traditional taxi drivers being 6.27, almost 13 times higher. An expert said, "People are usually less worried when their children take a taxi alone instead of using an internet ride-hailing service. But in fact, the latter is a safer choice."

Wang Xiaolin, who is a lawyer, said it's not reasonable to stop all teenagers under 18 using ride-hailing services when they do have such needs. "We can divide them into more specific groups. According to the country's law on road traffic safety, children under 6 cannot use public transportation without an adult. It's the same when it comes to car-hailing services," Wang said, "But the company should be able to let guardians know the real-time driving route to ensure children's safety," he added.

38. According to the survey, what do over half of the participants agree on?

(　　)

    A. Passengers' age should be restricted.

    B. Teenagers should take Didi rides with adults.

    C. Parents should be responsible for their children.

    D. Strict management of drivers is more important.

39. According to a report in 2018, what is a better choice for a safer ride?

(　　)

    A. Traditional taxi.

    B. Ride-hailing service.

    C. Public transportation.

    D. Not mentioned.

40. Which of the following can be more reasonable according to a lawyer?

(　　)

    A. Divide teenagers into more specific groups.

    B. Encourage children to use public transportation.

    C. Ride-hailing services should be banned to the public.

    D. Stop all teenagers under 18 using ride-hailing services.

41. What might be the best title for the passage? (　　)

    A. Who should be responsible for teens' traffic safety?

B. A successful ride-hailing company in China.

C. Should teens be allowed to use ride-hailing service alone?

D. More and more teens prefer ride-hailing service.

E

Google has launched a new app designed to help blind people explore their surroundings（环境）.

The free app, called Lookout, was first announced in May 2018. Now people in the United States who own a Google Pixel device（设备）can use the app. The company says it hopes to bring Lookout to more devices and countries soon.

The app uses technology similar to Google Lens. That product uses machine learning to recognize text and objects through a device's camera. Users can then receive information about the text and the objects. Lookout builds on the same technology, but aims to provide help to people who are blind or have low vision. The app uses a device's camera to recognize text and objects and then provide voice descriptions about what it sees.

Lookout is not designed to describe everything, but instead tries to search out things that people would most likely care about. The app can learn to tell what things are most important to a person over time.

Google says the app operates best when the user wears a device around the neck or inside a pocket, with the camera lens pointed outward.

Lookout has three main settings for people to use. The Explore setting is designed to help people carry out daily activities or identify things in new places. A Shopping setting can get products and help users identify their money. The Quick Read setting can help users go through their mails, read signs or identify other printed materials.

Google says the goal of the app is to provide more independence to the nearly 253 million people in the world who are blind or have serious vision problems. There are also other apps designed to help these people, like Microsoft's free Seeing AI app.

42. What can we know about the app Lookout? (   )

A. It is popular all over the world.

B. It can be used in all cell phones.

C. It is designed to help blind people.

D. It can describe everything.

43. What is special about Lookout, compared with Google Lens? (   )

A. It can recognize texts.

B. It can identify objects.

C. It can give voice descriptions.

D. It needs to work with a camera.

44. Which setting can be used if a blind man wants to read a medical report? (   )

A. Explore.

B. Shopping.

C. Quick Read.

D. Seeing AI.

45. Where can we probably read the article? (   )

A. In a diary.

B. In a storybook.

C. In a travel guide.

D. In a science magazine.

附录四 访谈提纲

学生访谈：

1. 你平时在家会阅读吗？

2. 你一般在家阅读多少分钟？

3. 你在家主要阅读什么方面的英语书籍？

4. 你最喜欢阅读哪一类英语书籍？

5. 你喜欢上英语阅读课吗？

6. 你觉得英语阅读课对你的英语学习有帮助吗？

7. 你觉得英语阅读课有趣吗？ 你最喜欢阅读课的哪个环节？

8. 你喜欢阅读课中老师的评价性的问题吗？比如，你觉得里面的做法对吗，为什么？

9. 阅读课里不同的问题，你最喜欢哪一类？直接回答型还是思考后再回答型？

10. 你认为你对文章写出不同问题的个数不少于10个吗？

11. 你喜欢老师的评判性提问吗？

12. 你喜欢评判同学和老师吗？

教师访谈：

1. 你是否平时会进行英语书籍的阅读？

2. 你擅长上英语阅读课吗？

3. 你的阅读课环节是否很紧凑？

4. 你的学生是否喜欢上英语阅读课？为什么？

5. 你觉得你上的最成功的阅读课的环节是哪个环节？

6. 较于常规课，你的学生阅读课的收获很大吗？

7. 你认为一节阅读课的教学目标应包括哪些方面？哪个目标最重要呢？

8. 你的阅读教学设计中主要培养学生的哪些能力？有关注到培养学生的批判性思维吗？如果有，怎样设计的？

附录五 研究工作流程

第一阶段流程图：

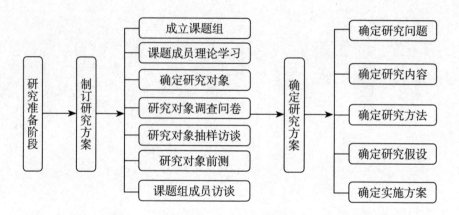

第二阶段流程图：

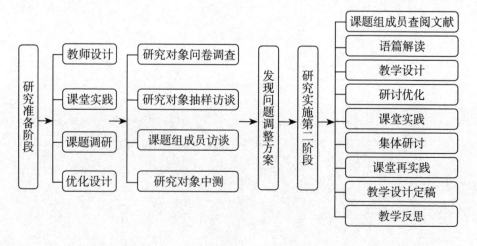

第三阶段流程图：

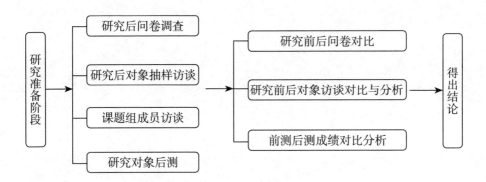

第四阶段流程图：

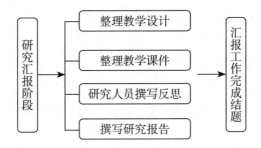